Praise for *The Cons*

Simon is one of the most consistent people I know and he's not only quali-fied to teach network marketers how to be consistent and be successful but also how to have a more fulfilling life.

—Ray Higdon

The Consistency Pill makes it easy for you to develop discipline with a simple 7 Step System. You'll learn how to overcome fear, develop emo-tional intelligence and discover time management tools and routines that you should implement. This book will play a huge part of your success and is a must read for every network marketer.

—Holton Buggs, CEO Ibuumerang

If there's anyone on earth best equipped to teach consistency it is Simon. Being friends with him for the better part of a decade now I can honestly say there is no better example of how to systematically make people feel seen, heard, loved and appreciated - consistently. The methods he uses to organize his approach are simple and effective. If consistency is your weak-ness, read this. Maybe you just need a system. Simon has one for you.

—Jessie Lee Ward, 7 Figure Earner

Simon is one of the most consistent people I know, but better than that, has helped countless of people around the world become super consistent. Whenever he creates content, I consume it!

—Frazer Brookes, Network Marketing Ninja, Social Media Trainer & Speaker

Having a "why" is not enough. That is why doctors go to medical school to learn skills. The best doctors? They concentrate in one area, and consistently improve their skills every day. Simon shows us how to follow their example.

—**Tom "Big Al" Schreiter, www.BigAlBooks.com**

This book is a must read for every serious network marketer. Consistency is what separates the average from the great. The book covers everything from the mental aspect to the day-to-day tools you can apply right now! The theory to practical application is key!

—**Daniel Song, 8 Figure Career Earner**

First…know that I LOVED the book…and READ IT HARD. I, like Simon, believe consistency is the MOST important trait a person can have. In life, baseball, and business. And *The Consistency Pill* finally nailed it for all of us! This book will bring everyone back to the center line of mastering skills and using them. I believe people will say after reading it that it was the booked that "turned on the light" for their success! Thank you, Simon Chan! For the book and the man you are!

—**Tom Chenault, Chief Sales Officer, Contact Mapping**

I think everyone would agree that consistency makes a difference. But for some reason, in this fast-paced society we live in, it is a rare quality. It is a blind spot for most people. But consistency pays the big money. After making my business decisions in a knee-jerk fashion for many years and coming out empty-handed each time, I finally realized that the missing link was my commitment and my consistency. I decided never to quit on a bad day. That's when things changed for me. Simon's book pulls it all together! This book represents the missing piece for most people driven to build a significant business in Network Marketing.

—**Jordan Adler, Network marketing millionaire, Author of the Amazon bestseller** *Beach Money*

Simon Chan is a brilliant and bold champion of the magic of consistency. *The Consistency Pill* is a powerful and profound work of art. Devour it, teach it and share it with your team. The results will be exponential.
—Richard Bliss Brooke, Mach 2 and The Four Year Career

In business as in all things, the ability to be consistent will trump just about every other attribute in the equation. In *The Consistency Pill*, Simon Chan hits this reality head on by offering the tips tricks and secrets that are the foundation of high achievers. Truth be told, he demystifies the process with articulate information that will not only accelerate success but minimize stress.
—Lisa Grossmann, Multiple 7 Figure Earner

Simon does excellent at determining the most important of all topics to discuss in *The Consistency Pill.* I've been building successful sales teams for the past 34 years with sales at the multibillion-dollar level and without any doubt consistency has been vital to my success. The book is simple to understand by Simon's perfectly placed pragmatic examples. *The Consistency Pill* is valuable at every level of the business spectrum (beginner or highly successful)… and it is also applicable to anything and everything one wants to get good or better at!
—Tim Sales, Founder of Network Marketing Power

The Consistency Pill gives you a system to make consistency a reality in your life. It's loaded with mental hacks, tips and routines that'll help you stay consistent and achieve success in your business.
—Marina Simone, Top Earner in Network Marketing + CEO of Moms And Heels™

Reading Simon's book is like sitting in a personal coaching call with him. You feel like he is imparting his wisdom directly to you and actually hearing all the excuses that swing through our heads as to why we do not do what we know will help us to have a successful business, and then hear Simon's voice overcoming those same excuses! I have been in our profession for over 35 years now, and my secret to success has been consistent in the activities that would move me further tomorrow than I am today. Simon delivers the 'secret sauce', the 'magic formula' in a way that is so simple to learn and more importantly, implement. Do yourself and your team a favor and make this a non-negotiable read. Simon is one of the most heart driven, servant leaders I know, and so I know he will have poured his heart and soul into this amazing gift to our profession.

—Celine Egan, CEO Juice Plus Aus/NZ

To succeed in anything, you have to take consistent daily action. In *The CONITENCY PILL*, Simon Chan distills decades of proven business building success into actionable, easy to follow steps that anyone can implement immediately to take their business and life to the next level.

—David Block, Founder & CEO, Previnex

Simon Chan has been there and done it. I've known him for many years now and he's one of the most consistent people I know. I've personally seen Simon apply his consistency and grow a very successful direct selling business in various countries. Anyone who wants to increase their online sales will benefit from this book.

—Robert G. Allen, #1 New York Times best-selling author

I have personally known and watched Simon for 15+ years participate and give back to a single industry and profession. The authority to speak about consistency can only be bought with action and time…. Simon Chan has paid in full.

—Soomin Kim, Top-Producing Real Estate Agent, Austin, TX

Everyone knows you can't be successful without consistency but often it can be difficult to stay consistent. *The Consistency Pill* will give you the tips and tricks to help you become successful in your business.

—Masa Cemazar and Miguel Montero, Pyjama Bosses, Trainers and MLM Software Creators

If you're not consistent you are starting over all the time I love what Simon shares in his book *The Consistency Pill*. Consistency is what so many lack if you could master what Simon talks about it will make a major difference in your success.

—John Haremza, Multi-million dollar earner, Author of *Right or Almost Right*

I've read many self-help books. This is truly an easy and simple read. A must for all small business owners who want to grow & take action.

—Brian C Chung, CPA, CA, Chief Home Officer, Personal Real Estate Corporation

I've known Simon for over 20 years and there's no better person to teach about consistency than him. *The Consistency Pill*, is full of real-life stories and lessons that you can apply to help you stay consistent and achieve success in all parts of your life.

—John Goerlitz, Million Dollar Club, #1 Customer Enroller, Independent Distributor Council

The lack of consistency is why most people fail in home-based businesses. Without consistency you'll never be successful. *The Consistency Pill* will finally allow you to stay consistent and make your dreams a reality.

—Robert Hollis, Author, Entrepreneur

Simon is one of my mentors when i started my business in 2009…and 13 years later… I've already made a 7-figure income several times and now have organization in at least 17 countries. I learned many things from Simon such as how he was a model of humility, his work ethic and his "one more" attitude. Doing one more meeting, one more presentation, one more training, etc. These are the things that really helped me build a huge business… but the biggest thing I learned from Simon was "consistency." I've known Simon for more than 13 years now and the first thing that will come to my mind when somebody mention his name is consistency. This guy has been consistent since the time I first met him! He's been consistent in all areas of life whether it's in business, social media, family, etc. and I admire him because of this. He is probably the most consistent person I know! I'm grateful to be able to know him as a mentor and a friend… Thank you Simon!

—Nathaniel Sunio, Million Dollar Club

This book contains the best techniques in all land for providing top sales systems, improve sales performance and unlock more revenue accordingly. After reading this book, you will feel that you too can accomplish anything you heart desires.

—Dede Hsu, Realtor

I've followed Simon Chan for many years and he's one of the most consistent people I know. He taught me that "Consistency is the Key to Mastery." *The Consistency Pill* gives you a simple system to stay consistent regardless of the challenges and distractions that you face every day.

—Jeff Street, Network Marketing Leader

The Consistency Pill is a simple to read book that gives you the mindset hacks, tools and system to help you stay consistent and achieve success in life.

—Steve Swartz, MilitaryToMillions.com

The Consistency Pill is a great step by step breakdown of what it takes to stay consistent in whatever you pursue in life.

—Angel Fletcher, 7 Figure Earner

In all my personal experience with Simon, it's always been framed with honesty, integrity, and respect. Those are attributes that I deeply respect.

—Larry Thompson, International Business Strategist

Simon is one of the best trainers and most genuine people that I know. He deeply cares for people, and because of that is willing to challenge them to become their very best. I highly recommend his training to anyone serious about grow their network marketing business!

—Bob Heilig, Virtual Upline

Everyone wants to be successful, but when push comes to shove, most LACK consistency. Simon is someone who I've admired for years, not just as a friend or collaborator, but because of his commitment to consistency! *The Consistency Pill* is a MUST read and easily breaks down EXACTLY how you can create more sales and success in your business by focusing on the ONE THING most are not. Stop overthinking and read this book!

—Brian Fryer, Social Media Expert & Best-Selling Author

Simon has always led the way when it comes to coaching and mentorship for Network marketers. If you are at all serious about producing results consistently to build the business of your dreams than Simon is definitely one of the best experts you can learn from!

—John Melton, Top 50 Global Earner, Network Marketing Hall of Fame

There's a great quote from Ralph Waldo Emerson that says, "what you do speaks so loudly I cannot hear what you say." Simon Chan is the epitome of this quote. He is the perfect person to write a book on applying consistency because he lives it as well as anyone I have ever met. This book will give you the blueprint for success. Read and apply these timeless principles into your lives.

—Rob Sperry, 8x Author and Public Speaker

The
CONI
TENCY
Pill

The
CONI
TENCY
Pill

The 7 Step System
to Increase Sales and
Transform Your Business

SIMON CHAN

NMTA
PRESS

Contact information for NMTA Press www.simonwchan.com

ISBN: 979-8-9850749-0-1 - Paperback
ISBN: 979-8-9850749-1-8 - ebook
ISBN: 979-8-9850749-2-5 - hardback

Ordering Information:
Special discounts are available on quantity purchases by corporations, associations, and others. For details, contact www.simonwchan.com

Table of Contents

Chapter 1: The One Thing All Leaders Agree On 1

    Why Consistency Matters 3

    Anyone Can Be Consistent 4

    The One Thing All Leaders Agree On 6

    How to Prevent Information Overload and Overwhelm 9

    Setting Goals Alone Is Not the Solution 9

    Your "Why" Is Not Enough 10

Chapter 2: People Buy Your Three C's 11

    People Buy Your Change 11

    Prospects Buy Your Commitment 12

    Prospects Buy Your Consistency 12

    Two Doubts That Every Prospect Has 13

    Most People Tend to Be Skeptical at First 13

    Social Media Makes Things Harder without Consistency 14

Chapter 3: Lucky Dave and How Success Starts 17

Chapter 4: The Mind Tricks That Work 23

    You Always Act the Way You See Yourself 23

    Let Go of the Past 24

    Bury Old Experiences with New Images of Yourself 25

    Change the Vision of Yourself 26

    Be Careful about What You Say 27

    How to Change Your Self-Concept 28

    I Always Find a Way! 30

    Remind Yourself of Your Past Successes 31

    Focus on Activity Instead of Results 32

Chapter 5: Consistency Beats Intensity 33

    The Wrong Way to Motivate a Sales Team 34

    Consistency Beats Intensity 35

    Take Small Actions That Create Lifelong Changes 36

    How to Keep Going When You're Not Getting Results 38

    Don't Make This Selling Mistake 39

    Frequency Is More Important than Duration. 39

    Take Small Actions Daily. 40

    Don't Let the Details Stop You. 41

    Your First 30 Days on Social Media 42

    Tackling Your Next Enemy 43

Chapter 6: The Experience Formula 45

    Our Lives Are Made up of Experiences 45

    Your Reactions Determine Your Experiences 46

    How Do You React?. 47

    Your Experience from the Event. 48

    How I Chose to React 48

    Apply the *Experience Formula* to Everything 49

    Five Tips for Reacting Better 50

    You Have the Power. 51

Chapter 7: How to Change the Outcome of Events 53

Chapter 8: The Rejection Killer. 57

    Every Business Goes through Rejection 59

    The Rejection Killer. 61

Chapter 9: Unlock the Power of Emotional Consistency 67

    Emotional Consistency Leads to Consistent Actions 70

Chapter 10: The Consistency System. 71

    The Seven Components of the *Consistency System*. 73

    Turning My Part-Time Business into a Full-Time Venture. 73

    You Are Already Consistent in Some Areas of Your Life 75

Chapter 11: The Forgotten Soy Sauce **77**

Be on Offense Instead of Defense 79

Focus on Activity and Not Results. 79

Scale Your Business by Increasing Your Team's Productivity 79

The DMO 3-5-5-5-3 Checklist for Home-Based Businesses 81

If You Don't Have Time to Work on a Checklist 83

Chapter 12: Create the Time **85**

Say "No" to Something You're Currently Doing. 86

Work in Small Chunks of Time. 87

Go "Watch a TV Episode!" 88

Schedule a Set Time Every Day 89

New Entrepreneurs Need to Treat Business Like a Job 90

Still Don't Have Enough Time? 91

Chapter 13: 10 Rules of the Consistency Productivity Regimen . . .**93**

Rule 1: Be a Defender of Your Time 94

Rule 2: 95% of Time Management Is Attitude. 94

Rule 3: Plan Your Week 94

Rule 4: Plan Your Day the Night Before 96

Rule 5: Plan Out Your Prospects 97

Rule 6: Always Have an End Time to Every Task. 97

Rule 7: Two-Second Rule. 98

Rule 8: Avoid Multitasking 99

Rule 9: Batching 100

Rule 10: Learn to Say "No" More Often 101

Taking the First Step Doesn't Need to Be That Hard 102

Chapter 14: The Game Plan. **103**

Make It Easy 103

Make It Simple 104

Make It Quick. 104

Three Rules to Follow 105

Chapter 15: Surroundings for Success. **107**

Change the People. 107

Use a Unique Location 109

Play the Same Song 110

How to Improve Quickly. 111

Chapter 16: Get 1% Better Each Day with This Tip. **113**

Tracking Creates Consistency 113

Tracking Your Sales Numbers and Conversion. 114

Track Your Time 115

Take a Consistency Huddle 116

Your Very Next Action Determines Your Success 117

Recap the Day and Focus on Getting Just 1% Better 118

Chapter 17: Your Consistency Toolbox **119**

1) Journal 120

2) Calendar 121

3) Timer 122

4) Time Tracker 123

5) Your Checklist. 123

6) Prospect List 124

7) Reading Apps 124

8) Gamification 125

9) Rewarding Activity 126

The Most Important Component of All. .126

Chapter 18: Action Through Accountability. **127**

Get Someone to Hold You Accountable. 128

Different Levels of Accountability 128

The Best Time for Your Accountability Call. 129

Format for Your Accountability Call 129

Putting the *Consistency System* into Action 130

Chapter 19: Singing Happy Birthday Every Day! 133

    Singing Happy Birthday Every Day 133

    Update the System to Accommodate Different Situations 136

    How I Wrote This Book 137

    Getting Back on Track 140

Chapter 20: Winning the Daily War 141

    It's a Daily War against the Devil 141

    Five Traps That Destroy Consistency 143

    How to Get Back on Track 145

    Putting It All Together 146

Chapter 21: Take The Consistency Pill 147

Acknowledgments 153

Works Cited 155

Additional Resources from Simon Chan .157

About the Author 159

CHAPTER 1

The One Thing All Leaders Agree On

We live in a special time in history. Thanks to the internet and the information age, anyone can be successful at anything.

If you want to learn about something and develop the skills to do it, all you have to do is Google it and you'll find helpful blogs, videos on social media, Facebook groups, or YouTube videos that will help you accomplish your goals.

And if you want to grow even faster, you can find a ton of affordable online courses that'll save you time and teach you more quickly.

All this was unimaginable even just 20 years ago.

Yet, with all these great resources out there, people are still stuck—and that's why I wrote this book.

I'm a shy, quiet Asian kid who grew up in Brooklyn, New York. As a kid, I was a huge baseball fan. My favorite team was the Yankees, and it was my dream to play professional baseball.

But there was one problem: I sucked at hitting. When kids would choose teams, they always picked me last because I was a terrible hitter.

If you follow me on social media, you'll know that one of my favorite things to do now is to practice baseball with my boys. I have also coached youth baseball for years, and all three of my boys are advanced hitters for their ages.

So, how did someone like me become qualified to coach and teach my boys to hit so well? They were definitely not "born" with their skills—in fact, they were lucky they didn't inherit mine!

I took *The Consistency Pill*.

When my oldest son fell in love with baseball, I saw it as an opportunity to spend quality bonding time while reliving my childhood memories. Just like any father would, I wanted to help my son do well and have fun.

I watched YouTube videos and identified all the mistakes that had made me a terrible hitter as a kid. I only wished I had had this free information at my fingertips when I was young!

My son loved baseball, so I invested in online courses and read a few books about hitting. I applied what I learned and started to practice with him every day after school.

Within the first week, he started to get really good.

With about four weeks of regular practice in the backyard, my son became the best hitter for his age in his league.

If you want to achieve extraordinary results, the good news is that all the information you need to know is out there.

All the knowledge that you ever need to be successful and live a life of fulfillment is available at your fingertips.

So, why are most people still stuck and struggling to achieve their goals?

Most people fail to achieve the lives they want because **they lack consistency.**

Learning the information from courses and videos alone didn't make my son great at baseball. He improved because we practiced every day at 3 p.m.

But consistency is not easy.

It's hard to focus when you're already busy with your job, being a parent, and nonstop distractions, or when you're just too tired after a long day of work.

Success can be defined in different ways, and in this book, **success is defined as achieving the income goals that you set for your business.**

People know they need to be consistent, but they don't really understand how important consistency is to success.

Many people think that just having a goal will help them become successful. Others may be excited after watching an instructional video or training course they purchased and think the knowledge alone will make them achieve what they want.

But *it's their level of consistency that will determine whether they will be successful.*

There are so many great trainings out there, but what's lacking is *The Consistency Pill.* It's the missing supplement to creating mastery.

I started my entrepreneur career in 2003, and consistency is what helped me become successful.

I've built a seven-figure business that had a global sales organization of over 200,000 distributors in over 18 countries, and in 2013, I launched one of the top business coaching companies in my industry.

The reason I was able to become successful is because of my consistency and how I was able to recruit leaders who also applied the same *Consistency System* in their sales teams.

My purpose in life is to have a positive impact on as many lives as possible, and I want to help you.

I'm going to teach you the same principles that I taught my business leaders and give you the *Consistency System*, so that you can increase sales and achieve the business goals you set.

Why Consistency Matters

I like to ask clients, "What do you think the number one skill you need in business is?"

Most people say the ability to network, sell, market, or handle rejection.

All of those are important elements of success, but they're not the *most* important.

The number one skill is consistency!

Consistency is the mother of all skills because *once you learn how to be consistent, you can get good at everything else.*

For example, even if you don't know how to create good social media content that attract prospects, if you just start posting for 30 straight days, you'll immediately get at least 10 times better. How do I know? Because that's how I learned, and it's how my coaching clients have mastered social media.

It's just like how, if you had never made sushi before but then made sushi for dinner for 30 straight days, you'd immediately become a pretty decent sushi chef.

If you become consistent, you'll be successful. It's as simple as that.

If you're reading this book, you're probably struggling to be consistent or feel you're not disciplined. Maybe you get bored or distracted and keep hopping around, trying to find the magic solution.

Regardless of your reasons, in these pages you'll learn how to be consistent and create mastery in whatever you want to achieve.

Anyone Can Be Consistent

Anyone can learn to be consistent. You don't have to be born with any special powers to figure out how.

How do I know?

Because I used to be very inconsistent.

I was a terrible student in college. I struggled to go to class every day and hand in my projects in time. The only thing I was consistent at was staying up till 4 a.m. playing videogames and skipping class the next day.

Unfortunately, my lack of consistency continued to hurt me when I started my career as an entrepreneur. It caused me to waste tons of time and lose money.

But fortunately, thanks to a mentor and the *Consistency System*, I was finally able to stay consistent, and I'll share the things that helped me.

What you'll learn are the exact strategies and tips that I teach my one-on-one coaching clients and the members of our amazing business community, *Purpose Driven Networkers*.

Something that keeps me fired up every morning is watching the members inside *Purpose Driven Networkers* get more consistent each day. From there, it's easy to see the improvement in their weekly results.

"Before becoming a member of the Purpose Driven Networkers, *I was really struggling with my business. I didn't know how to use social media. I couldn't stay focused on my recruiting, nor get new customers, and I was having trouble concentrating on my business. I attended trainings and focused on personal development, but nothing seemed to work.*

Since I've been a member the past few months, my business has grown. I've changed personally. I've learned how to be consistent with my personal life and my business. It's been a game-changer for me."

Jasmine McKinney (St. Louis, Missouri)

"Thank you, Simon Chan. Your simple 15-minute DMO is helping me a lot. I can talk to more people in a short period of time using your strategy, and it gives me confidence each day."

Fostine Ndlovu (Tzaneen, South Africa)

"This week, I had my best $$ week in this industry since I started with Purpose Driven Networkers *nearly two years ago. I still have a long way to go, but I appreciate Simon teaching me the*

importance and value of being consistent."

Taylor Hampton (Cuenca, Ecuador)

"Purpose Driven Networkers has definitely given a new meaning to consistency. Because of Simon's daily trainings, I'm more aware of my posture and mindset.

For the first time in my business, I have friended and enrolled a cold market Team Builder in only one week's time. Before, it could take months to close.

I've also added approximately 200–240 people to my friends list since joining Purpose Driven Networkers *three months ago."*

Miriam Groff (Windsor, Colorado)

"You've really helped me to take action—not just to have goals, but to actually take action."

Tracey Hulick Chapman (Nashville, Tennessee)

If you don't develop the skill of consistency, it's easy to waste time and money pursuing something that you'll never achieve.

The One Thing All Leaders Agree On

Don't believe me? I've interviewed over 700 top business leaders on my podcast, and even though everyone has their own unique way to create success, they all agree that consistency is the most important skill involved.

Consistency helps you master anything you want to pursue.

Any strategy will work if you become consistent.

Take the following, for example:

A University of Florida professor taught a photography class and split the class into two groups of students (Clear, 2018).

The first group of students were told to submit as many photographs as possible. (They were the "Quantity Group.")
Their grade was determined by how many pictures they sent in. If, by the end of the semester, they submitted over 100 photographs, they would get an A. If they submitted over 90, they would get a B. Over 80, they would get a C.

The assignment for the other group (the "Quality Group") was to study and submit their *best* photo by the end of the semester. They could only submit *one* photo.

Which group do you think became better photographers?
What the professor discovered was that the students who submitted the *most* photographs (the Quantity Group) became far better!
The same applies to your business.
You learn and become good at something when you do the same thing over and over again.
Thanks to the flood of free information online, a big problem now is that many people spend tremendous amounts of time on learning how to do things without applying it. They read books, watch YouTube videos and Facebook Lives, and attend events, but they never take the time to take action on what they learn. They just become self-development junkies and "learn, learn, and learn," when, in fact, they never really learn anything because they never apply what they were taught.
Most new entrepreneurs need to get on a *Personal Development Diet!* Instead of learning more and more, you need to take action and master what you've learned rather than jumping onto the next new thing.
If you don't take action, personal development *hurts* you more than it helps you because it overwhelms you with too much information

and often serves as an escape from doing what you really should be doing.

I'm not saying personal development is not important. It is, **but the learning is actually in the *doing*.**

My point is that you have to make sure you implement what you learn instead of overwhelming and confusing yourself by continuing to learn more things that you don't take action on.

One of my friends, who has earned over $50 million in his different business ventures, *never* finishes reading a book. Instead, the moment he learns something new, he puts the book down and makes sure he implements what he's learned within 30 days. That's been the secret to his success.

Let me give you another example of a time when you have to get on a *Personal Development Diet*.

I cannot cook well, but if you were coming over to my house next week and I wanted to make you the best dinner I could, what should I do? Watch 30 YouTube videos about cooking and never actually cook, or watch one video about the basics of cooking and cook for seven straight days?

Cooking for seven straight days will make me a much better chef.

But here is something many people don't consider.

Which plan would help me cook you a better meal?

Plan A: Learning to cook different dishes every night
Mon: Learn to make beef with broccoli
Tues: Learn to make beef fajitas
Wed: Learn to make sushi
Thurs: Learn to make lasagna
Fri: Learn to grill a steak
Sat: Learn to make fish tacos
Sun: Learn to make chicken marsala

Or…

Plan B: Learning to cook the same dish every night

Mon: Learn to make beef with broccoli

Tues: Make beef with broccoli again

Wed: Make beef with broccoli again

Thurs: Make beef with broccoli again

Fri: Make beef with broccoli again

Sat: Make beef with broccoli again

Sun: Make beef with broccoli again

With Plan B, I would be able to cook you a pretty good beef with broccoli by the end of the week!

In the process of cooking the same dish every day, I would have actually learned how to cook that dish well enough to never look at a recipe for that dish again.

We learn when we do the same thing over and over again. It may be boring, but that is how we become great. *Consistency creates mastery!*

How to Prevent Information Overload and Overwhelm

Have you ever been overwhelmed after attending a training session and not known where to start?

That's why it's much better to watch one video on cooking than it is to watch many and get overwhelmed.

Additional training is good, but it only helps after you've taken action and mastered something before you move on.

Setting Goals Alone Is Not the Solution

Have you ever been frustrated because you failed to reach your goals? You thought you did everything right by defining your "big why" and even employing the "S.M.A.R.T." rule of goal-setting:

S: Specific

M: Measurable

A: Achievable
R: Realistic
T: Timely

You did all that, yet you *still* fell short?

Setting goals alone rarely works for most people. In order for your goals to succeed, there has to be a consistency system in place to support them.

For example, if you want to lose weight, just setting a goal to go to the gym and eat healthier won't be enough.

You have to take action and create a new routine to support your goal. That is all part of the *Consistency System,* which we'll discuss later.

If you want to get in shape, you need that *Consistency System* for exercising and eating. That way, with consistency and time, you will hit your weight-loss goals. The same thinking applies to your business.

If you analyze your life, there's a *Consistency System* behind anything you regularly do, whether you know it or not. Whether it is brushing your teeth first thing in the morning, exercising, or taking a shower every day, there's a routine behind it.

Your "Why" Is Not Enough

Just like goal-setting, having a "Big Why" or a big reason to do something is not enough if there is no *Consistency System* behind it.

I'm going to teach you how to increase sales and make more money in your business.

If you want to be a successful entrepreneur, you have to know how to sell, and **the most important thing you must sell is yourself.**

Whether you're selling a vision or a product, you must sell yourself. But how do you get someone to buy when you don't have much of a track record?

You're about to discover the three C's that'll help you create a following and get people to buy from you.

CHAPTER 2

People Buy Your Three C's

Every entrepreneur must be good at selling themself.

Whether it's selling your vision, your product, or your service, ultimately, people are buying you. They buy you if they feel they know you, like you, and trust you.

But how can you sell that if you don't have a previous track record of success?

Every leader started out with nothing at one point. Fortunately, you'll be able to convince people if you understand that…

People Buy Your Change, Commitment, and Consistency!

Let's talk about what this means and how you can apply it.

People Buy Your Change

If you want to get people's attention, the first thing you must do is change yourself.

This can be a change in your attitude, habits, lifestyle, a positive result from the products you're selling, or really anything else caused by your consistency in action.

Change gets people's attention and impresses them. It also makes them curious about what created this change.

Prospects Buy Your Commitment

Your commitment also gets people's attention. They start noticing that instead of relaxing after normal work hours and doing what everyone else is doing, you commit extra time to your business and vision.

Instead of sleeping in on weekends, you get up early for workshops.

This type of consistent commitment convinces them that you have something exciting going on.

Prospects Buy Your Consistency

Ultimately, your change and commitment can't be short term.

A common business question I get is, *"How do I convince people?"*

The answer is, *"Don't convince people. Outlast them."*

In most cases, they'll say *"No"* the first time, simply because the timing isn't right for them.

But if you're consistent with following up, eventually *every* prospect will be a customer or will give you a referral. Seriously. Every person! Even if the person doesn't like what you have to offer, they'll respect your consistency and they'll refer you to someone to help you out.

Consistency convinces people because otherwise you would have quit.

People are often skeptical because they see many people get excited about things, only to lose interest quickly and give up.

Here are some examples:

▼ A friend is excited about their new home gym equipment but stops using it after one to two months.

▼ An acquaintance goes out and gets a real estate license, only to never sell a house.

▼ Someone joins a home-based business but quits after three months.

But, if you stay consistent and keep doing the same thing over and over again, this will convince prospects that whatever you're selling is good. Otherwise, you would have stopped.

Two Doubts That Every Prospect Has

If you have a business or you're in sales, you have to understand that every prospect has these two doubts.

The first doubt is, *"Is this for real?"*

The second is, *"Will you help me?"*

What prevents people from buying *you* is your lack of consistency.

Your prospects believe, trust, and respect what you're selling based on your level of consistency.

You can't be selling one thing one day and then doing something else the next.

Who's going to trust a salesperson if one day he's saying how great Mercedes-Benzes are, the next week he's talking about life insurance, and today he's talking why it's a good time to buy real estate?

People ask themselves, if the product or service you're selling is *really* that good, then how come you're not consistently selling it every day?

Don't make them doubt you.

Show up every day like the other "million-dollar businesses" they see, such as McDonald's, Starbucks, etc. Not only are those business always open, but they also sell the same thing all the time. You don't see them switching menus often.

If you're not consistent, your prospects automatically don't respect you or what you're offering. In their minds, you don't have a good product, because otherwise you'd be working hard at selling what you're selling every day.

Most People Tend to Be Skeptical at First

People out there are used to seeing people quit, so that's why they're skeptical when you have something to offer. It may not be something personal against you, but they've just been conditioned to be skeptical because they know most people are inconsistent and stop doing what they start.

However, when people see your consistent change and commitment, that's when they will believe that you're for real.

The "three C's" will make you stand out and look like a winner.

People become impressed with people who don't quit.

Some of my best business partners were people who stood on the sidelines watching me in my first year. It was only after they saw me doing the same thing over and over again that they took a serious look at what I was offering.

So, that's why consistency is what holds change and commitment together and makes everything work.

Only the winners and champions stay consistent long-term, and everyone wants to join a winner.

Social Media Makes Things Harder without Consistency

In the days before social media, you could show up every once in a while, and people would be impressed. If you slacked off for the rest of the week, who would know?

But now, everyone is watching you.

Once you meet someone, there's a great chance that they're checking you out online.

I'm very active in youth baseball, and at one point I was coaching three youth baseball teams *at the same time*. Coaching kids and making a positive impact in their lives is something I'm really passionate about.

I live in Southern California, where it's always warm, so our season starts in late January. Every year, I always find new people "stalking" me on Facebook.

If you've ever seen the "People You May Know" suggestions that Facebook shows you, those people are clicking on your profile even though they're not your friends.

LinkedIn also lets you know how many profile views you're getting and who is checking you out.

When I go see who's clicking on my profile in late January, it's always the parents of the kids I'm coaching for that season.

Why?

Because these parents wanted to make sure that they can trust their kids to their coach. They want to know what I do for a living. They want to know about my hobbies, and they want to make sure that I won't be a negative influence on their children.

I see this happen in business as well. Every time I speak at company events, I see a ton of new people checking out my social media profiles.

The same is happening to you.

Most people have at least a Facebook, LinkedIn, Instagram, TikTok, or Twitter account, and they're clicking on your profile and checking you out.

Are you consistent with your social media? Are you showing prospects your commitment?

Don't worry if you haven't been consistent up until this point. You can get started now.

When I was in college, I rarely went to class and would always sleep in because I would be up late every night playing video games.

But then something changed in my life. Let me take you back to a cold winter night in December of 2003.

CHAPTER 3

Lucky Dave and How Success Starts

My personal journey as an entrepreneur began when a friend of mine recommended I read *Rich Dad Poor Dad* by Robert Kiyosaki.

At that time, I had a job that I liked. It was low pay, but I enjoyed the perks, and I thought I'd stay in the company forever and slowly climb the corporate ladder.

I wasn't aware of other paths I could take, like being an entrepreneur and not having to be stuck at an office all day, so *Rich Dad Poor Dad* totally opened my eyes to exciting possibilities.

Once I read it, I realized I couldn't afford to stay at my job and work the nine-to-five. I was like a bird out of a cage, one that would never fly back.

I wanted a business that would allow me to live a life of flexibility and freedom. I didn't want to be stuck in one geographic location or have set working hours. More importantly, I now wanted passive income! That's income that continues to pay you even when you're not working, such as income from collecting royalties or rent money.

But I thought to myself, what business can a shy, quiet Asian kid from Brooklyn be successful at?

I immediately thought of opening a Subway franchise because they were very popular at the time. But the problem was that I didn't have the money to get started, and I didn't want to be stuck working at the restaurant seven days a week.

So, I read more books to find a solution.

I read Kiyosaki's *Cashflow Quadrant* and Robert Allen's *Multiple Streams of Income*. That was how I learned I could generate a good income and create a flexible lifestyle with home-based businesses.

I got excited!

High-speed internet had finally become widely available at that time, and it was possible to run a profitable business without having a storefront or employees!

Just around the same time, I also read *The Purpose Driven Life* by Rick Warren.

God is very, very important to me, and I felt that whatever I chose to do, it had to have God's blessing.

After reading that book, I realized that God's purpose for me was to have a **positive impact on as many lives as possible.**

I've always liked to help people. In college, I was a counselor for the youth group in my church. I also enjoyed running basketball clinics at the YMCA in New York City's Chinatown and encouraged kids to study and work hard instead of hanging out on the streets.

Once I discovered my purpose in life, I realized that choosing a home-based business where I could help and empower others was what God wanted me to do. I did some research and chose a profession that required me to constantly help people, which fit in perfectly with my purpose.

I said to myself that if long-term success in my venture depended on how many people I helped, then God must want me to do this.

So, that's how I got started as an entrepreneur in 2003.

Since I'm a fitness fanatic and was already buying shakes and vitamins at GNC, I decided to market nutritional supplements.

I researched and found a company that I would be happy to partner with. No one ever approached me. I just went to Google and typed in that company's name and "Los Angeles," found a random person, and reached out to him.

Let's just call this guy "Lucky Dave."

I left a voicemail, and Lucky Dave called me back the next day. It was probably the easiest sales call he ever had!

The fact that I went to a stranger's website to purchase a business starter pack immediately taught me the importance of online marketing, and was one of the reasons I made the decision to be an online marketer in 2004.

Despite how easy it was to get started, parts of the business were really hard.

Not only am I an introvert, but I had also just recently moved to Los Angeles and didn't know many people. Most of my friends still lived 3,000 miles away in New York, and this was way before online videos and webinars were available.

I struggled for months, and I didn't know why. I knew the business model was great, and I had done the research. A few months in, I had already invested over $2,000, but I hadn't made one penny back.

Then, one winter night, I was staying over at my parents' house in New York. I went to hang out with some of my friends in the city, and, as I pulled up to my parents' driveway, something happened.

I was listening to a business training audio that I had downloaded and burned onto a CD. A six-figure income earner named Steve was talking about how great our profession was and I was thinking, *Yeah, yeah. I've heard that before.*

And then, he said something that smacked me right in the face.

He said, "If you do this home business on a Monday, and then take two or three days off, and then do it on a Thursday and then take two or three days off because of the weekend, and then on Sunday you feel guilty and hate going to your job, so you do the business a little bit, it's never going to work for you! You have to do the business every single day, or you will never make it."

And when I heard that, I was like, *Wow!*

I felt like he was talking directly at me!

That was the reason I was struggling. I had *no* consistency!

I realized I needed to show up every single day and prospect. There are many forms of prospecting to generate sales, such as calling people and sending out text messages, emails, etc., but I was not doing any of them *consistently.*

From that night on, I started to prospect with a new will and drive. But in spite of my new dedication, I still wasn't seeing results because I still wasn't consistent. It's hard to be self-motivated when you get rejections.

It's all too easy to slack off when you don't get the results you want. Rejection drains your emotions and kills your motivation to keep going, and I found myself struggling with consistency again.

And then, one phone call on a Friday afternoon changed everything.

Lucky Dave called me and said that our team leader, Steve, wanted to work with me!

I was like, *"Is this the Superstar Steve who does all the trainings that I listen to?!"*

When he said yes, I couldn't believe it!!

I had never met this guy, but I listened to his trainings every day in my car ever since that aha moment I had in my parents' driveway.

Supposedly, Steve was looking for someone new to work with closely, and Lucky Dave had said a few good things about me. I had no idea why Lucky Dave was impressed with me, since I was struggling big time.

Maybe it was because I hadn't quit yet, or maybe it was because I was the easiest sale he had ever made and he wanted to help me.

Anyway, within a few minutes, I was on a three-way call with Lucky Dave as he introduced me to Steve.

I was starstruck and shocked and kept on thanking Steve for mentoring me. All he asked me was whether I really wanted to be successful, and I said, "Heck yes!"

And then he told me to stop kissing his butt and get ready to work like

I had never worked before in my life.

I had no idea what I was getting myself into.

This was the first time I had had real accountability, and I didn't like it.

Within the first week, I couldn't stand Steve. He would *never* leave me alone.

He would force me outside my comfort zone and make me talk to people I didn't want to talk to. He'd also never accept any of my excuses, and just refused to listen to my explanations if I told him I couldn't do something.

I couldn't hide from him, either.

Steve would text me or call me multiple times a day and kept asking me what the heck I was doing.

He drove me nuts!

Even though I couldn't stand him, it was the best thing that could have happened to me at the time.

Why?

Because *we all need someone to hold us accountable* if we want to be consistent, and this is one of the reasons I started *Purpose Driven Networkers,* a business community for home-based business owners.

One of the main things that we do in the *Purpose Driven Networkers* group is that everyone gets to prospect together with me on Zoom. The reason I do this is because you're more consistent when you do things with others.

Steve held me accountable and set the right expectations for me. He told me that, even if I didn't have any skills, one out of 100 prospects would buy.

Knowing that fact gave me hope. I knew I would be able to make sales and grow a successful business.

Once I started tracking the people I talked to, I would get excited every time someone told me "No" because that meant I was one step closer to that 100 prospects.

Now that I had a mentor holding me accountable, I had to create a routine so that I could have something good to report back to him each day.

At the time, I was working a job in the sports industry. My work schedule allowed me some free time at 4:30 p.m., so every day at that time I would spend 15–30 minutes on my income-producing activities.

At first, I was so scared and bad at prospecting that I could only go for five minutes, but eventually I got more comfortable and was able to prospect for up to 30 minutes before I had to go back to my full-time job.

And before you know it, I had "accidentally" created all seven components of the *Consistency System,* which you'll soon discover in this book.

Once I took action, my self-esteem improved, and I wanted to see if I could prospect even more.

I went back to my calendar and found that I could fit some prospecting time into my lunch schedule, as well as five to 10 minutes during my coffee breaks.

Even if a break just gave me enough time to leave one voicemail, I would make sure I did something during every break just to "stay in the game" and not get rusty.

I stuck with this *Consistency System,* and **consistency creates mastery!** I slowly started to get a few sales, and three months after Steve held me accountable, I earned my first $1,000 weekly check.

I continued to stay consistent and use what I'm about to teach you, and eventually I reached the top 1% in my profession.

I recruited over 80 people a year for over five years, but it wasn't easy. I'm human and constantly distracted, but fortunately, the *Consistency System* helped me stay consistent.

If you get easily distracted like I did, how can you stay consistent every day?!

Let's go to the next chapter and I'll teach you the first steps to becoming consistent in anything you do.

CHAPTER 4

The Mind Tricks That Work

**Your attitude and mental approach matter most
when you face the challenges thrown at you.**

Now, I know it is tough to be consistent.

You're not a disciplined person, you get distracted easily, or you may even have ADHD.

I understand your frustrations because I was the same way.

I'm the person who can't read for more than 10 minutes without my mind starting to wander, but once I applied this strategy, I was able to read more than 50 books a year.

You Always Act the Way You See Yourself

The first step is understanding that we always act the way we see ourselves.

How we view ourselves is called your self-concept (Ackerman, 2021).

If you see yourself as a good mother, you'll want to do everything you can to be a good mother. If you consider yourself physically fit, you're going to exercise even on the days when you don't feel like it. If you feel like you're a healthy eater, you'll do your best to eat healthily. If you view your-self as someone who is not really into healthy eating, you'll find yourself eating a lot of junk food.

Since you always act according to the way that you see yourself, you have to *stop* seeing yourself as someone who is not consistent.

Instead, you must ***start* seeing yourself as someone who *is* consistent!**

But how can you do that if you don't have a track record of success?!

Let Go of the Past

You can't start seeing yourself as consistent if you allow your past to hold you back.

I'm always teach my coaching clients that you must let the past go and remind yourself each day that:

Yesterday is history, today is a mystery, and tomorrow is my legacy.

Start seeing yourself as the *new* you.

Why?

You're already a new you because you're reading this book!

Each word that you read is changing you. Every new idea you read and everything you're learning is creating a new you!

I want you to start seeing yourself as the new you, as someone who gets more consistent each day.

If you start seeing yourself this way, the magic will happen and you'll start actually becoming more consistent every day.

How does this magic work?

It's because the way we act mirrors how we see ourselves!

And here's the coolest part. *You* get to make the decision of who you want to be. There's no one out there who says you're born a certain way and have to be like that for the rest of your life.

You can *change!*

All it takes is for **you to make the decision** of how you see yourself and who you want to be.

Instead of seeing the way you've been, I want you to start seeing yourself as your *future* best self.

This applies to everything in your life.

I see myself as a great father, and because of that, I find myself doing things for my children even when they're expensive, tiring, and inconvenient. The only reason I go out of my way to do those things is because I see myself as a good dad.

Change your self-concept and you'll change your life.

Bury Old Experiences with New Images of Yourself

I know you're thinking, *"How can I simply let go of all the times I've failed to stay consistent?"*

Unfortunately, our brains are not like computer hard drives where we can just reformat and delete everything, but there is something we *can* do.

We can always cover our past negative memories with new experiences and future images so that the past becomes dimmer and dimmer, to the point where we start forgetting about the negative memories.

Here's an example of how it works.

We have all gone through events in our lives, often in high school, that we thought were the "end of the world." These events could be first breakups, times we failed major exams or didn't make the sports team, etc.

In those moments, we were emotionally crushed, and that's all we thought about.

But you probably barely remembered your "end of the world" moment until I just brought it up.

Why?

Because so many other things have happened since that event. You've focused on different things, and all the new events and experiences have buried that memory.

You can start doing the same thing right now to your "failures"—burying them with new experiences.

What you focus on is what stays in your mind.

Start seeing yourself as consistent and successful, and you'll soon start remembering these new images and forgetting your past events.

You can be the *new* you now, and the first step is to start seeing yourself in the future.

Change the Vision of Yourself

I'm sure you've heard leaders talk about their visions for what they want to accomplish, but there is an important part of vision that many people don't spend enough time talking about.

It's the vision of the future *you*. Do you have a clear image of your best self in the future?

If you want to be a business leader who impacts thousands of people, do you see yourself on stage motivating others?

If you want to be a top sales recruiter, do you see yourself winning all your company awards?

And most importantly, *do you see yourself as the* most *consistent person you know?*

What is your vision of yourself?

You may have a vision of how big you want your sales team to be, the lives you will change because of your business, or what lifestyle you want, but you probably aren't spending enough time visualizing who you will become.

You need to start seeing yourself as the leader on stage who's empowering people and, most importantly, as the *most* consistent person in a room.

You can find a picture of a top business leader giving a presentation and then look at that picture every day. However, instead of seeing that leader, use your imagination and visualize yourself giving that presentation.

Start seeing yourself as your future best self and you will act that way.

Now I know it may be difficult, but you will get better at it each day. It starts with the words you use.

Be Careful about What You Say

Your self-talk and what you say to yourself creates the image of how you see yourself.

Let's say there are two people who want to quit smoking.

Someone offers the first person a cigarette, and the person replies, "No, thank you. I'm trying to quit."

Someone offers the second person a cigarette, and this person says, "No, thank you. I'm not a smoker."

Which person do you think has a greater chance of quitting?

Obviously the second one, the person who doesn't see themself as a smoker (Clear, 2018).

Here's an example you can start using right away:

Instead of, "I'm trying to be consistent," say to yourself, ***"I'm getting a little more consistent each day."***

The second focuses on your progress and motivates you to become more consistent each day.

"Trying" also never works because, by using the word "try," you're telling yourself that you may not make it. You're giving yourself a way out. You either do something or you don't.

I always use this example when I speak at business conferences and company events. I get everyone to stand up and then have them "try" to sit down. After a few seconds everyone laughs because you can't "try" to sit. You'll end up standing or squatting!

One of the ways to get yourself to become the person you want to be is to stop using the word "try."

Pay attention to the words you use because they play a huge role in determining who you'll become.

How to Change Your Self-Concept

I'm going to give you a few simple steps to change the way you see yourself.

Step 1: Say to yourself repeatedly throughout the day, *"I'm a consistent person."*

Start the morning by saying that and repeat it throughout the day.

Step 2: Find examples in your life where you are consistent.

These examples don't need to be business-related.

Maybe you kiss your spouse each morning or hug your kids every morning, or perhaps you wash your car every week.

Step 3: Stop seeing yourself as struggling because, if you're struggling, that explains why you're not getting the results you want. See yourself as a successful person and do what a successful person would do instead.

I want you to start seeing yourself as someone who is consistent, mentally tough, and willing to do things that most people won't do.

I want to share a story about someone who did one-on-one coaching with me:

When Adeline first applied for help, she was struggling in her business and couldn't sell. Her fear of rejection made her inconsistent and prevented her from making any sales and getting people to join her team.

Even if she was finally able to get the courage to talk to someone, she would sabotage herself by thinking about her lack of success and how she had struggled for years. Her lack of confidence and her negative opinion of herself scared away all potential sales.

The first thing I do with my one-on-one coaching clients is to work on their self-image and how they see themselves.

I told Adeline to list out the characteristics of a successful business leader and to start acting like that person. I reminded her that most successful entrepreneurs also get nervous and have fear, but they visualize success and act in spite of that fear.

After I taught her this, I would message Adeline every day to make sure she spent time visualizing herself being a top leader and acting like that leader.

As the weeks went on, Adeline was able to stay consistent despite her fear and slowly started to get results. Within three months, not only was she able to stay consistent and get new sales, but her sales team started to follow her and duplicate her results.

Step 4: Do one small thing each day that you didn't really want to do.

It can be as simple as doing one push-up that you didn't want to do.

That small thing doesn't need to be hard, but this step is very important.

People often tell me that I'm the most consistent person they know because once I start doing something, I show up every day. Whether it's my abs workout, my daily motivational Consistency Pep Talks on social media, or MLM Nation's podcast, I make it a habit to do things that I've committed to even when I don't want to.

Someone asked me the other day how I'm able to make myself do certain things even though I don't feel like doing them.

I replied, "Because I'm the type of person who's consistent and mentally tough, so I keep going even during the tough times."

I'm not born more discipline than people who are less consistent, nor smarter, but I see myself in a different way.

Instead of complaining or wimping out, I like to take on a challenge.

I don't let too many things get to me or get me down. I'm only able to do that because I see myself as consistent.

If you have a hard time seeing yourself in a different way, then you can start building up that confidence and image of yourself by doing small things you don't want to do.

The thing you don't want to do might be reading one more page after you start to get bored.

It could be taking a one-minute walk when all you want to do is sit down and relax.

It could be finishing one more lap around the track or making one extra sales call after you want to stop.

Do something small that you don't want to do, and that will slowly build up mental toughness and change the way you see yourself.

It'll also reinforce and prove to you that you are indeed getting a little more consistent each day.

I Always Find a Way!

The last thing I want you to do is to adopt this mantra: *"I always find a way!"*

This is something I learned from someone who was very successful. No matter what challenges he came across, he said to himself, "I always find a way!"

This mantra has helped me tremendously as I run a company while doing my best to be a good father at the same time. It seems like every time I have a good work routine down, I'm thrown off track again because of my kids.

With school and all of my kids' extracurricular activities, their schedule constantly changes every three months. It can be very frustrating, but ever since I adopted the "I will always find a way!" mantra, I always figure out a new schedule that works. My mantra forces me to be resourceful and resilient and to never give up.

If you say, "I always find a way" to yourself all the time, believe it or not, you'll automatically start making things happen.

You may not be able to solve every problem in your life immediately, but you'll be solution-oriented, solve way more problems, be more consistent, and be more successful.

Remind Yourself of Your Past Successes

Affirmations are positive statements that you say about yourself over and over again, such as, "I'm the most consistent person I know."

Can you change yourself simply by saying affirmations?!

No. Affirmations are important, but you have to do a few more things as well, or you won't be able to change your self-identity.

This is what you need to start thinking about and focusing on.

First, focus on any small successes you've had in your life.

One thing that has helped me tremendously is to focus on the sales that I've made in the past instead of the sales that I have lost.

When I first started, I would keep a PDF copy of the completed application for my first business sale on my desktop to remind myself that, if I could make one sale, I could make another. That kept me going when I had to go through a series of rejections and "noes."

Even if you haven't been successful in business yet, you've had success in other areas.

Maybe you're a parent, have a successful career, or play sports well, or perhaps you're good at video games.

I'm sure you've been successful in *something* in your life, and that means you can also be successful in what you're doing now.

You don't need to have had "massive success" or have been the smartest kid in your class or the best athlete. You just need to have had small wins.

Let me give you some ideas of what "small success" can look like.

Small success could be your kids running to you, happy to see you when you come home. That's a success that many people wish they have.

Getting started as an entrepreneur is also a success because you decided to change your life instead of just settling for an "average" life.

Reading this book is another success because most people don't do any personal development. So, you're already more successful than they are.

Stop being so hard on yourself and focus on the small wins you've had.

One of the things I work on with my coaching clients is I have them list out at least 20 successes they've had. Maybe they've bought a new home, had their first child, cheered their kid on as they graduated from school, or gotten through a personal crisis.

I want you to list out your successes.

Focus on Activity Instead of Results

Second, focus on activity instead of results. If you focus on results, you're going to get let down. You're going to be disappointed.

Your identity will change if you take small actions.

If you make your bed consistently, guess what? You can start seeing yourself as someone who is very neat and consistent.

You don't need to exercise for a long time, but if you just exercise for a little while each day, your self-concept will change.

This works if you exercise for just five minutes a day or even just for one minute a day, every single day!

Does it really matter if you exercise for just one minute a day?

It matters because you start seeing yourself as someone who is consistent and healthy. Someone who doesn't see themselves that way wouldn't take the trouble to go to the gym for just one minute.

These small actions make you start seeing yourself as consistent and will lead you to be consistent in other areas of your life.

The opposite is also true. There's a popular trend called "Challenges" (such as a 90-day weight-loss challenge to see who can lose the most weight) that can hurt you more than help you.

Be aware of this marketing hype and avoid these activities and programs. Even though the creators of "Challenges" have good intentions, you'll soon discover why they rarely work and why they cause more harm than good.

CHAPTER 5

Consistency Beats Intensity

Everyone knows taking action is important, but most home business owners either don't get started or mentally quit after a few days because they don't believe they can be successful.

You already know how important your self-concept is.

The way we act is always consistent with how we see ourselves, and our identity will change if we take small actions.

You don't need massive action nor results to start becoming consistent. You just need small actions to get started.

That's why it is *super* **important to start small.** Make it simple and easy to get started because taking small steps changes the way you see yourself and increases your confidence.

A common mistake that I've seen new home business owners make with social media is that they try to do too much too soon. They're new and never really posted consistently before, yet they want to be on every platform (Facebook, Instagram, LinkedIn, TikTok, etc.) immediately.

They then easily get overwhelmed, discouraged and stop.

What would be easier is to start small and just focus on posting once a day on one platform to create confidence and momentum.

The opposite is also true.

Hard challenges will make you procrastinate and will hurt your self-concept. You should avoid them, especially if you're struggling to be consistent.

You see examples of this in exercise, weight loss, or sales activity challenges. Many of them require you to do intense activity for seven, 30, or even up to 90 days!

For most people, it's almost impossible to complete challenges that require you to do something intense for a long period of time.

I still remember the popular P90X exercise program a few years ago, where you had to work out like a maniac for 90 days. My first reaction when I saw that program was that there was *no way* I'd be able to do that for 90 days! The program was so hard that I wouldn't even want to do it for *one* day, let alone 90!

These challenges are harmful because they hurt your self-concept. Instead of helping you see yourself as getting more consistent each day, they reinforce your belief that you can't do the thing that you're trying to accomplish.

The Wrong Way to Motivate a Sales Team

The worst way to motivate a sales team is to create a contest where most don't think they'll be able to finish, let alone win.

Many direct selling companies and sales leaders make this mistake. I've witnessed and also personally participated in many selling contests that fail to achieve their goal to get more people to sell more.

Business leaders who hope to motivate their entire sales teams often make the mistake of giving out huge prizes, hoping that the prizes will get more people to participate, but it rarely works. The prizes tend to be based on who gets the most results instead of who does the most activity.

The people who the leaders hope to motivate don't even bother to participate because they know they have no chance of winning.

What ends up happening is that the same sales superstars, who don't need the extra motivation to begin with, often win all these challenges.

When the average salesperson sees the same leaders winning all the time, it destroys their confidence and reinforces their negative self-concept that they're not good enough and can't do it.

If you've been struggling with consistency, make sure you avoid these intense challenges because they do more harm than good. Instead, start with small action steps and focus on your activity instead of results.

Consistency Beats Intensity

Success is rarely because of "one big hit." Instead, it's about consistently doing small things over and over again.

Bill Gates created Microsoft only because he spent all his high school days programming while other kids were out having fun.

The Beatles played every night at no-name bars before they became an "overnight success" (Gladwell, 2008).

Jerry Seinfeld did stand-up comedy to small crowds for at least five nights a week to create his success (Comedy Central, 2015).

Every successful person focuses on taking consistent actions every day.

But more importantly, *consistency always beats intensity* because of how it changes the way you see yourself.

As I get older, I don't push myself in the gym anymore, and I'd consider my workouts to be pretty wimpy.

I don't push myself hard nor do any of the crazy hard workouts that you see many people do online.

Yet, I'm in decent shape.

Why?

Because I do some type of exercise every single day.

I might do the wimpiest workout, I might give only 25% effort, but I still show up every single day, rain or shine!

One of the secrets to my success is that I understand that *consistency beats intensity.*

Intensity doesn't last and often leads to burnout. Someone who is consistent will always beat someone who can't maintain intensity because no one looks forward to intensity! You can do it for a short time and then burn out.

For me, if I do one hard-core, intense workout at the gym, I'm already dreading the next time I have to go back! And often, I just don't.

But something light and easy will allow me to stay consistent and keep coming back again and again.

The consistency in exercising is also more important than the intensity, because these light workouts reinforce my self-concept and make me see myself as someone who is consistent and cares about my health.

You have to understand that everything is a "muscle" and the way you see yourself is like that.

The more you use your consistency muscle, the stronger it gets, just like how, if you'd never exercised before and just started doing push-ups every day, you'd get stronger.

The more you do a simple action, the better you get at it and the more you see yourself as the person who does that action.

So, even if you just sent out one message to a prospect every day, you'd start seeing yourself as a more consistent person and a more successful leader.

These small actions will start making you treat the business seriously and you'll become more consistent.

Take Small Actions That Create Lifelong Changes

Growing up, I struggled with low self-esteem and my head was filled with negative self-talk.

English was my third language, and I grew up in a mostly Caucasian neighborhood. I was picked on because I didn't understand what people were talking about!

When I played the game "Simon Says" in kindergarten, I would always lose. Sports were also hard for me because of the language barrier.

I saw myself as a wimpy kid. I wanted to win, but I couldn't.

Back then, I saw myself as mentally and physically weak. Today, I see myself in a totally different light.

So, how did I change?

I used small actions to change the way I saw myself.

I'll give you a few examples.

When I used to play basketball with my friends, I would stay for five extra minutes to practice shooting free throws after everyone left, even though I was dead tired.

I would run outside in 25-degree weather in the snow for 20 minutes while most of my friends would stay in and play video games.

The more I did this, the more my self-esteem increased because I was able to do things that others weren't motivated to do. I saw myself as tougher, having better work ethic and more drive.

And the more I did those activities, the better I got at sports, and the more my self-concept slowly started to change.

This continued into my business career.

One of the best pieces of advice I got from one of my mentors was to take cold showers.

Now, what do cold showers have to do with business?

They help you with mental toughness and delayed gratification.

There are so many proven benefits to cold showers (Watson, 2017), and they feel so good afterward, but the first 20–30 seconds are brutal.

People think I'm crazy, but I just see myself as consistently mentally tougher than them. I say to myself that I'm the type of person who can handle short-term challenges and won't let anything stop me.

Another one of my routines is to hang on a pull-up bar for two minutes immediately after I wake up each morning.

I'm not doing pull-ups nor chin-ups—I just hang on the bar for 120 seconds—but it still hurts!

Go try it if you've never done it. I guarantee that it'll hurt your hands and, if you're like I was when I started, you won't even last 30 seconds. Your fingers and forearms will hurt, and you'll get calluses very quickly.

But you'll eventually get better and better at it.

I hang on the pull-up bar not to get stronger, but because it makes me see myself as someone who is consistently mentally tough. I can make myself do things that I don't want to do each day.

It increases my confidence to know that, if I can withstand the pain of the pull-up bar or the painful experience of cold showers, then I can handle whatever challenges come my way that day. I can step outside my comfort zone because I've done it already.

We're our own biggest enemies. These two activities give me a quick win before the day even starts.

I know I have conquered myself and can take on whatever challenges come on that day.

How to Keep Going When You're Not Getting Results

Your efforts and work are never wasted, so it's important that you focus on the activity rather than the results. This is even more important if you start anything new. If you focus on results, you will be disappointed and be tempted to quit.

People who never become successful think that because they're not getting immediate results they're failing.

You're not.

Success and consistency are like melting ice.

Think of this situation.

You're sitting in a freezing cabin that is only 23 degrees. You have an ice cube in front of you.

You start a fire to heat up the room, but nothing happens to the ice.

Is your effort wasted?

You throw more logs onto the fire to make it hotter. Now the temperature is at 25 degrees, but still nothing happens to the ice cube.

Is your effort wasted?!

You put more logs onto the fire and now it's at 31 degrees. Still, *nothing* happens to the ice cube.

By now, you've worked up a sweat throwing the logs on the fire.

Is your effort wasted?!

Of course not!

That's because, when the room finally hits 32 degrees, the ice will melt.

But the temperature won't hit 32 degrees without your consistent effort.

None of that is wasted work—and the same applies to your career.

Your efforts are not wasted if you've been consistent in your income-producing activities and not getting results. You learn along the way, and your self-concept also changes. You have to stay consistent and keep going.

The key is to focus on the *activity* and not the result.

Don't Make This Selling Mistake

A common mistake that new salespeople make is that they focus on "quality" prospects. They spend so much time looking for the perfect person that they don't talk to enough people to get good at prospecting.

I'm not saying qualifying prospects is not important. You definitely don't want to waste your time with the wrong people, but you should approach *everyone* and then decide quickly whether they're qualified or not. You sort fast. Unfortunately, most people don't even start sorting because they're constantly overthinking and procrastinating.

Talk to lots of people and sort fast. Focus on talking less to *more* people, and you'll get good fast.

Frequency Is More Important than Duration

Another mistake salespeople make is focusing on the amount of time they spend working on a business.

The *number* of times you do something is more important than the *amount* of time you do something.

That's why our *Purpose Driven Networkers* get results when we prospect together. Each prospecting session is only 15 minutes long, but we have sessions multiple times a week, and the consistency creates results.

Focus on the activity and not the results. For example, focus on how many reach outs or how many follow-ups you do, rather than on how many sales you make as a result of those actions.

It's better to spend 15 minutes a day on something for seven straight days than it is to work on it for three hours and not touch your business the next day.

Even if you just do one call, that's better than none. Going to the gym for just one minute is better than not going. Wimpy workouts are better than no workouts. Sending just one message a day is better than nothing.

This applies to other things in life as well. Spending 15 minutes talking to your children every day is more important than talking to them for three hours on a weekend but not checking in with them during the rest of the week.

Take Small Actions Daily

Small actions increase your self-esteem and change the way you see yourself.

Your activity defines the person *you* become and will help you see yourself as a serious business leader. The more you see yourself this way, the more action you're going to take.

Before you know it, you'll create a nice positive cycle that'll make you better and better.

I want you to create a routine where you can take small actions in your business every day.

A small action can be sending just one follow-up message during your lunch break or sending out one initial message in the car before you drive home.

You can send one follow-up text before you step into the office at work, create one social media post before you go to bed, etc.

Don't Let the Details Stop You

Make sure you don't let the details stop you from taking these small action steps.

For example, you don't need to overthink the best filter to use to make the perfect social media post. That perfection trap will make sure you never hit publish.

Even if you think something is perfect now, when you look back at it months from now, you'll realize it was terrible because of how much you've learned and grown since then.

When you first get started, don't focus on perfection. The quest for perfection comes from your mental conditioning and how you were brainwashed in school not to make mistakes.

In business you have to make mistakes, and version 1.0 is always better than version 0.0.

When you focus on perfection, in the beginning all it does is create procrastination. Just get started, and you can make improvements later.

As long as you focus on an activity, the details and mastery will eventually come.

I'll share something personal with you about my business journey.

If you follow me on social media and especially on Instagram, you'll notice that I create new content every single day.

A seven-figure earner I coach recommended the app Over.

I started playing around with it. Now I've been using it for a year, and I still don't know everything about it!

I just discovered something the other day that totally changed things, and I was so excited about the new possibilities. I would have never known about it nor discovered my style if I hadn't been using Over every day for six months straight.

When I look back at the first images I created with the app, they weren't that good.

But that doesn't matter. What matters is that those images got me *started*.

Another important thing to realize is that most people don't remember your old stuff if you consistently put out new material.

If you've been following me on social media, you probably don't remember every piece of content that I created three years ago. People don't even go back a few weeks. They just remember what you do *today*, and that's why being consistent *today* and what you do *today* matters most.

Your First 30 Days on Social Media

Remember that we learn by doing!

If you take small actions over and over again, you're going to get good.

The photography students who submitted the most pictures beat out the ones that focused on quality. You get better at something by doing it over and over again.

Apply this to your business and with social media.

Most people who don't get immediate results on social media quit posting after two to three weeks.

You need to post on social media consistently for at least 30 straight days to get some type of traction, and it can take up to six months before you see a big jump in sales (Snow, 2015).

If you focus on getting immediate results with social media, you're going to be disappointed. You're not going to get quick results, and, if you do, it will be because you just happened to have gotten lucky.

Your goal for the first 30 days of posting is *not* to get results but to *discover your voice and your style,* so focus on the activity and the results will eventually come.

When you implement what you learn, you gain knowledge, and it is the knowledge and experience that will make you win in business—not more "learning."

The more action you take, the more you learn, and most importantly, the more you'll start seeing yourself differently.

Tackling Your Next Enemy

You already know that most of success comes down to your mindset and how you approach things.

We all have a common enemy: ourselves. We are in a constant battle against our negative self-talk.

You've already learned lots of tips to help you change the way you see yourself by visualizing your best self, taking small actions every day, and not letting perfection hold you back.

Now it's time to tackle your next enemy, your emotions.

A lot of the stuff you've learned is easy to say but hard to do because of our emotions.

Emotional detachment to outcomes is difficult, but the ***Experience Formula*** will allow you to conquer your negative emotions so that you can stay consistent.

CHAPTER **6**

The Experience Formula

If you want to be consistent in your actions, you first have to be consistent with your emotions!

Your business journey is full of challenges and rejection, and if you let your feelings alone determine what you do, then you'll never be consistent. You can't let your emotional state alone determine your actions and ultimately your success.

That is easy to say and hard to do because we're human, but there is something that'll help you stay emotionally consistent.

You can use my **Experience Formula** to overcome challenges and prevent unfavorable events from stopping you from becoming consistent.

The **Experience Formula** will show you that you can *control* your life and that you have the power to decide whether to live a happy life that is filled with wonderful experiences or live a life of misery.

Our Lives Are Made up of Experiences

We can define everything that happens to us as an "Event."

For example, if someone doesn't reply back to your message, that is an Event.

If someone says something unkind to you, that is also an Event.

For most people, if they have desirable Events, they're happy, and if they have unfavorable things happen to them, they become sad, frustrated, or angry.

They can become victims of what happens, but it doesn't need to be that way.

My *Experience Formula* is that it has *nothing* to do with the things that happen to us and everything to do with *how we React to what happens to us.*

Your Reactions Determine Your Experiences

Here's the formula that will change your life:

$$\underline{\textbf{Experience} = \textbf{Event} + \textbf{Reaction}}$$

An **Event** is something that happened to us.

The **Reaction** is how you respond to what happened to you.

Your **Experience** is the outcome you have in your life, whether it is success or failure, wealth or poverty, health or illness, happiness or frustration.

My *Experience Formula* reminds us that you cannot control the **Events** that happen, but you have the power to determine your **Experience** by choosing how you **React**.

If you focus on how you'll **React** instead of focusing on what happens, then you'll have a happier and more meaningful life.

Unfortunately, most people focus on what happens and not on what they can do. You see this all the time when people complain about or focus on problems instead of spending their energy finding solutions.

It's pointless to focus on **Events** because you have no control over them.

In other words, "don't cry over spilled milk" or else you'll make the mistake of complaining and making excuses.

Accept whatever has happened and move on by focusing on the best way to React.

I'll give you an example from when my oldest son was almost three years old.

I went to pick him up from preschool one day and he was so happy to see me that, before the teachers could stop him, he jumped down from a two-foot ledge on the school playground. Unfortunately, he landed badly and was yelling in pain.

When my son was still in tremendous pain 10 minutes later and wasn't interested in eating or listening to his favorite Thomas Train songs, I feared what had happened to me as a child had happened to him.

Having been on crutches four times in my life, I know a bad accident when I see one. I knew my son must have injured his leg badly.

I had a similar bad injury in a basketball game when I was younger and ended up fracturing my left tibia. So, I took my son straight from school to the Emergency Room, and, three hours later, my fears were confirmed.

He had fractured his right leg and would have to be in a cast for six to eight weeks!

After I made sure he was okay and feeling better, the shock of what had happened settled in.

Our family trip to San Diego for the weekend had to be cancelled.

My son wouldn't be able to go to school for the next few weeks.

My quarterly meetings for my business had to be postponed, and all my plans for Monday had to be cancelled.

On top of all that, I would need to find someone else to help my son during the next six to eight weeks.

My son breaking his leg was an **Event** that I could not control. I couldn't blame him for being so happy that he jumped down to see me.

But what about the teachers who could have stopped him?!

Should they be responsible?!

How Do You React?

The next step in the formula is my **Reaction.**

$$\text{Experience} = \text{Event} + \text{Reaction}$$

When I heard the diagnosis from the doctors, I could have Reacted angrily and blamed the teachers.

Yes, the teachers may have been partly responsible, and technically the school was liable since the accident had happened on school property.

However, my son had run and jumped down so fast, could they really have stopped him?

I could have Reacted by making a case against the school or by being bitter that they hadn't put up a barrier so that kids couldn't make that two-foot jump.

However, what would my end **Experience** been if I did that?

Your Experience from the Event

If I had blamed the teachers and gotten angry at the school, I would just go home furious and bitter.

I would most likely be so angry that I wouldn't even be comfortable sharing what happened with you.

If I had made a case against the school, it would have cost me a lot of valuable resources such as time, money, and physical and mental energy, all resources that would be better spent on my son.

If I had responded with regret, questioning myself about not getting to my son more quickly, about whether I could have prevented him from jumping, I would still be unhappy now, replaying the scene in my mind over and over again.

In either of those situations, I would have had a terrible **Experience** and brought unhappiness and regret into my life. Those Reactions wouldn't have made my life more fun and enjoyable.

How I Chose to React

The way that I chose to respond to the situation was to tell myself that things in life happen. I saw the next few weeks as additional bonding time with my son.

I would have to carry him more.

I would have to pat him more to soothe him, to make him feel better.

I would also have to take more time to give him baths because I had to wrap his leg in a plastic bag and towel so that his cast wouldn't get wet.

I love my boy, and I knew many unique memories would be created.

And that is exactly what happened.

Until the day I die, I'll always remember how I carried my son into the X-ray room and explained to him how X-rays worked.

I'll never forget how I held his hand to soothe him and tell him not to be afraid of the big machine that would make "clicking sounds" as each X-ray was taken.

I'll treasure the moments when we sat at the kitchen table and played with Play-Doh, since he couldn't run around and play with his trains.

I couldn't control how he jumped and fractured his leg.

I couldn't control what the teachers or school could have done.

I could, however, control how I **Reacted,** and I turned this unfortunate Event into a new, wonderful father/son bonding **Experience.**

Apply the *Experience Formula* to Everything

You can apply my *Experience Formula* to anything that happens in your life.

If you're in sales and face rejection from your prospects, you can't control that, but you can control your response.

If you React and say that this business doesn't work and no one else will have any interest in it, then your Experience will be bad, and you will be unsuccessful.

If you React that way, it'll be hard to stay consistent because you'll want to avoid the negative Experience.

But if you React by seeing your failures as learning Experiences, then you can ask yourself, *How can I be better next time, and what skills do I need to learn?*

That will give you a positive Experience. You will learn from your mistakes and be better the next time, and this will motivate you to stay consistent.

Five Tips for Reacting Better

The key to the formula and our ability to control the life we want to live is how we **React.**

If we React the wrong way, we will have a bad Experience and be unhappy.

If we respond properly, we will have a better Experience and even learn a few lessons in life.

Here are five simple tips for how to React better:

1) Accept That Events Happen in Life

Sometimes we get dealt good cards, and sometimes the hand is not as good.

That is just how life is.

We can't think that we are "unlucky" or "lucky."

If you've been lucky your entire life so far, sooner or later you will be "unlucky," and vice versa.

You can't undo things that have happened.

The only thing you can do is make the best of what has happened and see if you can prevent negative **Events** from happening again.

2) Always Be Grateful for What You Have

Gratitude is the easiest way for us to be happy each day.

Appreciate what you have.

If you think you have it bad, just look around you and you'll notice that others have it worse.

Gratitude always prevents you from being negative.

3) Never Criticize, Complain, nor Condemn

When you're negative, you only get negativity back because *you automatically start focusing on problems instead of solutions.*

You may temporarily prove yourself to be right, but your overall **Experience** will be negative because you will be blind to the solutions and lessons from the problem and your life will be miserable.

4) Stop and Think before You React

See if you can catch yourself for a split second before you respond.

That is what awareness is about, and the more you can find yourself thinking before you React to something, the more logical and less emotional your responses will be.

Emotional responses are rarely the right responses.

Just think back to the last time you were angry at a friend and said some hurtful words.

Your emotions (anger) made you say something you regretted later because your words had no logic to them.

5) Always Look for the Lesson

Successful people look for the lesson in everything negative that happens to them.

They don't dwell on the negative nor live in the past, because they know that we learn the most from our challenges.

The best use of your mental energy and time is to think about the lesson in whatever happens, so that you can prevent a negative **Event** from repeating.

What things can you do differently in life to prevent such Events from happening in the future?

You Have the Power

Remember that you can't control **Events,** you can only control how you **React,** and that ultimately determines your **Experiences.**

You have the power to create the **Experiences** you want. You can turn a negative into a positive, and this allows you to stay consistent.

To make the *Experience Formula* even easier, let's turn the page and have some fun in the next chapter as we learn to magically change "bad" **Events** into "good."

CHAPTER 7

How to Change the Outcome of Events

With the *Experience Formula,* your **Reaction is important** because if your **Reaction** is poor, you'll have a negative Experience and vice versa.

Here's the secret to having better **Reactions.**

Your perspective and how you interpret what happens (the **Event**) can make it easier or harder for you to have good **Reactions.**

A few years ago, I taught at one of my full-day *NO BS NO HYPE* direct selling training events in Melbourne, Australia.

After the event, I was at the VIP reception, and two of the attendees came up to me. One of the men introduced me to his business partner and told me how proud he was of him.

I asked the man why and he told me he was proud because his partner had still shown up on time at 9 a.m. even though he had a *really bad* night.

I asked the man this question: "Is it really a fact or just an opinion that something *really bad* happened to him last night?"

His partner was surprised at my response and the man repeated that it was *really, really bad.* I replied back saying that he might get mad at me for saying so, but it was just an opinion.

The man emphasized to me, *"No. It's a fact. It was really bad."* So, I asked him what had happened.

He said, "Someone broke into his home at night and robbed him at gunpoint. They made him open his safe and stole everything he owned. That's pretty bad! But he still showed up for your event."

I told him that it was impressive that he had still showed up, but saying it was "bad" was still an opinion and not a fact. It was "bad" according to him, but not to everyone.

Then he and his partner got a little annoyed and he raised his voice and said, "How can being robbed at gunpoint not be bad?! That's a fact! That's bad!"

I told him that the idea that what had happened was bad was just an opinion and not a fact because, to the Marine who had just stepped on a landmine and lost both legs in battle, his partner had a very easy day. The Marine would wish to trade places with him. He had a good day compared to that Marine.

He immediately got it and realized that his "bad" was just an opinion and not a fact.

I added that others would say he had a *lucky* night because he was robbed but not killed. He wasn't physically harmed and was able to attend my event the next day.

At that point, he and his partner understood that how we define things are opinions and not facts.

It's important that you understand this, or else you'll overanalyze and give wrong interpretations to the things that happen to you in your business.

When things happen to you, you need to ask yourself whether your perception of what has happened is a fact or opinion because it's important not to make emotional decisions.

It doesn't matter what business you're in, you want to be logical and rational. When you act out of emotion, your decisions are almost always bad ones.

We are humans though, and we tend to overanalyze, overthink, and misinterpret situations. That causes us to feel down or get discouraged.

A simple way to give yourself a correct perspective on the things that happen to you is to constantly ask yourself, *"Is this a fact or an opinion?"*

When you ask this question, it challenges you to think deeper and realize there's always another way to look at things that'll encourage you and help you stay positive instead of making you feel down.

When you just blindly label something as "bad," you fail to see the potential benefits of what happened.

If you understand that things that you consider to be unfavorable are simply opinions, you allow yourself to see things from another perspective. Often the answers to your problems are revealed when you approach things differently.

The "bad" things that have happened to you are often the best things that happen in life. **They're wake-up calls that bring what needs to change to your attention.**

For example, is it really "bad" if someone doesn't watch your sales presentation video even after they say they'll watch it?

"Bad" is only an opinion. In this case, you've just saved yourself time prospecting the wrong person.

Is it really "bad" if your team member quits after one month?

That's only an opinion because it's actually good that you avoided wasting time on training a person who would quit so easily.

Was it really "bad" that it took me 42 people to get my first sale?!

I thought it was bad until I realized that was just my opinion, and that I was actually better than some new entrepreneurs! It was also good because it allowed me to deal with rejection better later on. Rejection no longer bothered me because I knew I had gone through 41 "noes" before. It made me mentally tough.

My "terrible experience" of struggling for months was also just an opinion. Looking back, it was the best thing that could have happened to me because it led me to realize that it was my lack of consistency that held me back. I was lucky to learn this lesson earlier rather than later.

Was it a "disadvantage" that I was a shy, quiet Asian kid starting a business that required me to be able to communicate well?

That's just an opinion, too. I can say it's an advantage because being shy and socially awkward forced me to build my business online in 2004 at a time when most people in my profession were still building their businesses face to face.

A successful business leader and a good friend of mine recently posted on her Instagram account. "Shoutout to the worst moments in my life," she said, because if it weren't for those moments, she wouldn't be anywhere close to where she is today.

All top leaders know how to see things from a different perspective.

Remember the *Experience Formula*:

Experience = Event + Reaction

Our **Reactions** to the **Events** that happen to us will determine our **Experiences.**

Stop labeling things as "bad" when you encounter unfavorable **Events.**

If you ask yourself the question, "Is it a fact or opinion?" then you'll realize that there's always another way to look at things and that everything is *good!*

You'll stay motivated, encouraged, and emotionally consistent.

However, I know that when you get constant rejection in sales, it can sometimes distract you or make you forget about the *Experience Formula.*

You're about to discover the *Rejection Killer,* which will help you overcome the negativity around rejection.

CHAPTER 8

The Rejection Killer

It was a Saturday in October 2005, and I was out in Kuala Lumpur, Malaysia, preparing for our company's launch in that country. I remember this as if it were last month.

I wanted to be a pioneer and open up the Malaysia market, and I was doing business presentations every day.

One day, I met a guy who was an agricultural engineer.

He showed up and signed up to become one of the first distributors in the country. He was really emotionally fired up!

A few days later, he arrived for his first group training at my apartment and showed the same excitement.

He had a great attitude, was very enthusiastic, and brought this special notebook with him, a really nice expensive one with a leather cover and nice paper stock.

After the training, he came up to me and said, "Simon, thank you so much for the great training!"

He then showed me all the notes he had taken and told me that my training was so special that he had decided to write about it in that special journal. Inside the nice leather-bound notebook were notes on all the most important things he had ever learned from his mentors. It also included his daily reflections and a diary of all the big events that happened in his life. He said that our business would change his life, so he decided to take what he had learned from our training and put it into his life journal.

Then he said to me, "I'm super excited, and I'm going to be your first person to hit seven figures in Malaysia! I'm going to go all out and make it happen. People are going to be so amazed!"

He then shared the big plans he had and how committed he was.

He kept on sharing his excitement and vision and was the last one to leave my apartment. Of all the attendees that day, he stood out the most because of his enthusiasm.

I had been an entrepreneur for about two years, and my inexperience led me to have high hopes for this guy. I was excited because I thought I would have my first superstar sales leader in this new market.

Twenty minutes after he left, my phone rang, and it was him again. He was down at the Starbucks below my apartment, and he was talking fast with excitement.

He said he had randomly bumped into one of his old friends who was very successful in business, and this friend was going to partner with him! He was super excited and kept talking about how he and his friend would soon be very wealthy.

At this point, I was a little cautious because I had recruited over 80 people a year and, in order to do that, you have to get a lot of "Noes." I had met many people who would say they would partner up but never did. I don't believe anything until someone actually takes action, but I did my best to encourage him and tell him to bring his old friend to our next group training on Wednesday night.

I was in a rush because I had another meeting to attend, but he wouldn't let me off the phone!

He kept telling me how excited he was and how he and his friend were going to be the first seven-figure earners in our company in Malaysia. I finally had to tell him that I really had to rush off before I missed my next appointment, and then we hung up.

Little did I know that that would be the last time I would ever talk to him.

I sent him a text the next day to see what had happened to his friend, and he never replied. I was busy with other sales meetings, so I didn't think much about him until a few days later. I was cleaning my apartment and found a notebook near the shoe rack. I immediately recognized it as the special leather journal that this guy had shown me.

My reaction was, *"Oh no! That guy left his special life journal!"* I didn't even want to open it, because I was afraid I would stumble on some personal stuff that I shouldn't read. I wanted to return the notebook to him immediately.

I called him, but he didn't pick up. So, I left him a text saying that I was just checking in on him and wanted to let him know not to worry about his special journal because I had found it in my apartment.

He never replied. I held on to that special journal of his for months, until one day I just threw it away.

Reflecting back, I know what happened.

He was super excited, but his friend and a few others probably rejected him and said "no" to his sales presentation.

His ego and pride also took a big hit, especially after he had told me how successful he would become, and he could never recover from that.

Unfortunately, many people are like him and don't stay emotionally consistent. They get derailed by rejection and never become successful.

Every Business Goes through Rejection

I was talking to someone last night, and she asked me if there was a better platform than Facebook for generating sales for home businesses.

She said the reason she was asking me was because she was getting tons of rejection on Facebook.

I told her that the problem was not Facebook, because if you go Instagram, you will still get rejections. If you use LinkedIn, you will still get rejections.

It doesn't matter what platform you use or where you live. Whether you're talking to strangers on the street, conference attendees, old friends, people at meet-ups, or even leads you generated through advertising, you will get rejections!

I told her that the issue is not the platform, but how she's handling rejection.

If you can't get over rejection, you're never going to be successful in any business because every business faces rejection.

Think about businesses such as grocery stores, where tons of people walk by every day and do not go in.

That's rejection!

But does the owner cry about it or think of relocating? No.

You must get over rejection and worrying about what people think about you or else you'll never be successful in anything.

If you are afraid of rejection or caught up in worrying about what others think of you, you will be inconsistent or fail to take action when you need to.

Caring about others' opinion of you is also a form of fear of rejection. You're worried that you don't fit in and that you will get rejected.

In sales, if you're not following up with people consistently, it's because of your fear of rejection. If you knew these people would say *"yes,"* then you would reach out to them immediately!

I'm sure you probably have a few people who you should be following up with. If I told you that all of those people are 100% going to purchase, but you must contact them within the next 30 minutes or they're going to buy from someone else, you'd put this book down and call them immediately! But the reason you procrastinate and don't call them is because you're expecting them to say "no."

Your fear of rejection and your worries about what others think also cause you to be inconsistent in showing up on social media. If you didn't care about others' reactions to your posts, then you would post whatever you wanted and not talk yourself out of greatness by overthinking.

*If you can't handle rejection and be in a consistent
emotional state, then you're never going to be consistent
in your actions to become successful in business.*

But how do you handle the never-ending rejection?!

It can be very discouraging, but you can overcome these feelings and *not* let rejection stop you with my *Rejection Killer.*

The Rejection Killer

My 10-step *Rejection Killer* will help you get numb to all the "noes" you'll get.

Step 1 is knowing that people are not rejecting *you.* They're saying "No" to the message, not to you.

Step 2 is about your mindset and changing your perspective on who loses when someone is not interested. The way you see things is very important.

This is something I use all the time.

I just remind myself that **it's their loss.**

If they're not interested, it's their loss.

The timing may not be right for them, but it's still their loss!

They have an opportunity to experience a great product or service and they just missed out.

It's their loss and not your loss!

Step 3 of the *Rejection Killer* is changing your self-talk to *"You don't need them, but they need you!"*

If they say *"No,"* it's their loss because there are millions of people out there for you to prospect on social media, and, even if you live in the smallest town, you still have a few thousand people you can approach.

You have tons of people you can sell to, but there is only *one* of you they can work with, and they lost out on their opportunity.

Step 4 of the *Rejection Killer* is realizing that you are doing *them* a favor when you prospect them. Most salespeople get it wrong and have it the other way around. They think the prospect is doing them a favor when they watch a sales presentation.

No! It's the other way around. You are doing *them* a favor—because not only are you sharing something that can help them, but, in many cases, if they buy, it's you who has to take the time to help them.

If you think they're doing you a favor, then you've lost posture and become needy. Your prospect will sense that and immediately be skeptical.

Step 5 of the *Rejection Killer* is visualizing success before you reach out to someone.

Many salespeople struggle because they visualize failures and lack of success. They're constantly remembering the people who said "no" to them instead of the successes they've had. If you expect people to not buy, then there's no motivation to stay consistent in your selling activities. You will procrastinate to avoid rejection.

Instead, you should visualize your past sales.

If you're new and haven't made many sales yet, then you should reflect on all the customers who have purchased the same product you're selling but from someone else.

The fact that you know there are buyers out there will put you in a positive mental state.

I always teach that things happen twice, first
in the mind and then in reality.

If you're thinking about the negatives, then you'll attract the negative because your prospect can feel the negative vibes. Your lack of confidence will turn them away. Even someone who is interested will get skeptical once they feel your lack of belief. Being positive doesn't guarantee you'll make the sale, but visualizing the negative will scare buyers off.

Step 6 of the *Rejection Killer* is going for high numbers and talking to as many people as possible in the shortest amount of time.

If you talk to only five people a week and all five say "*No,*" then the rejection is going to hurt. But if you reach out to 50 people a week, those five "*Noes*" won't bother you as much since you have 45 other people to follow up with that week!

You can't spend all day talking to just a few people.

You need to talk *less* to more people.

Remember that you're the messenger and you have to get that message out to as many people as possible in the shortest amount of time.

In our *Purpose Driven Networkers* business group, we prospect together 10 times a week, and many of the members do at least 10 follow-ups online in just five minutes. The one to two "noes" don't hurt as much because they still have seven to eight people they have to follow up with before the day is over.

Step 7 of the *Rejection Killer* is realizing you get paid for every "no" you get.

How does that work?

This is some of the best advice my mentor taught me. He told me that even if you're totally clueless and not sure what you're doing, one out of every 100 people will be a customer or want to work with you.

That means if you earn $100 for every sale and you need to reach out to 100 people before someone buys, then you earn $1 for every "no" you get.

Once I discovered this, I would make it a game to see how many "noes" I could get each day. If I got seven, then I made $7. If I pushed myself hard and got 15 "noes," then I earned $15. I made it a game and it helped push me to take more action and get numb to the rejection

The cool thing about this game is that, if you track your numbers, you'll get paid more and more for each "no" as your skills get better and you stay consistent on social media.

I eventually improved and was able to sign up one person for every 10 people I talked to, so I made $10 for every "no" I got.

You must track your numbers to make this game work.

Step 8 is tracking your numbers.

Track how many new contacts you meet each day, how many people you invited to look at what you have to sell, how many follow-ups you did, and how many people watch your presentations.

Tracking is important because it encourages you. It lets you know when you'll arrive at your destination and get your signup.

It's like the GPS in your car.

What's the first thing you do when you get in a car for a long road trip?

You put the address in your phone and look at the time it takes and your time of arrival!

Imagine if you were just driving for hours without knowing when you'd get to your destination!

The trip would get very boring and you'd get frustrated. But when you know your estimated time of arrival, it motivates you and, as you get closer to the arrival time, the GPS (tracking) also encourages you to stop less and drive faster.

It's the same with prospecting and why you must track your numbers.

Tracking will also show you how you improved over time. The fulfillment of seeing yourself get better gives you more reason to keep going.

Step 9 of the *Rejection Killer* is meeting new contacts all the time. This helps you talk to high numbers of people.

When you have a constant supply of new leads coming in, then you no longer have the pressure to close a person because you have no one else to talk to.

One of the biggest mistakes that salespeople make is that they
don't go out to meet new people until they run out of prospects.

The worst time to meet new people is when you have to make a sale. That's when you tend to get more desperate and needy and the rejection hurts more.

The best time to meet new people is when you have plenty of other people to sell to. You can just focus on the relationship-building and not be emotionally attached to any result.

This is why meeting at least five new contacts a day is an important part of *The DMO (Daily Method of Operation)* sales checklist that I will share later on, in Chapter 11.

Step 10 of the *Rejection Killer* is training yourself to get numb to rejection with this simple game. I taught this to our *Purpose Driven Networkers* and one member immediately got 10% off his dinner!

The game is called "Asking for 10% Off" and is as simple as this.

The next time you go out to buy anything, ask for 10% off when you get the bill.

It could be the next time you order coffee, go out to eat, etc. Just ask for 10% off.

If you're like me, you're going to be super scared and stressed the first time you do this, but then you realize you're scared because of your fear of rejection.

Most people will say "*no*" or give you a curious look, but afterward you'll discover you're still alive and nothing bad has happened to you! The only thing that happened was that you got mentally tougher and learned to become numb to rejection.

I often ask for 10% off, and 80% of the time I'll get a "*no*" with a weird look. I just say, "I figured today might be my lucky day, so I thought it doesn't hurt to ask" and smile.

Or sometimes I'll say, "I come here a lot and was wondering if you do anything for loyal customers," and often I end up with a 5% discount.

Make sure you realize that the purpose of this game is not to actually get a discount but to develop your numbness to rejection.

The goal of the game is to get *more* rejection, so you become numb to it.

Remember that everything is a muscle, and the more you use a muscle, the stronger it gets. This applies to your resistance to rejection.

The more times you get rejected, the more you will develop numbness to rejection, and this will make you stay consistent with your prospecting. This will also help you close more sales because you'll learn to be bold and confident when you ask for the sale.

You'll realize that the worst thing that can happen is...nothing!

Everything in your business will become more fun and easier as you get better at handling rejection.

The greatest success and fulfillment you'll get is seeing how you grow as a person. And there's one evening routine that will make your life journey even more rewarding and fun.

CHAPTER 9

Unlock the Power of Emotional Consistency

Everyone has heard of IQ (Intelligence Quotient), but in many ways your EQ is even more important.

EQ stands for Emotional Quotient. Just as IQ measures how smart you are, EQ measures your ability to manage your emotions in a positive way so that you react better to what happens. This helps you relieve stress, communicate effectively, empathize better, overcome challenges, and defuse conflict.

You can increase your EQ so that you stay consistent emotionally and on track, regardless of what happens.

Here's my mantra that helps me stay emotionally consistent:

> *"Don't get too low when things are bad and don't get too high when things are good."*

That's important to remember because the truth is that when things are bad, they're never really that bad, and when they're good, they're also really not that good. So, don't get too high and don't get too low.

But we are human and not robots, so how do we get over those emotions?!

My *Daily EQ Quiz* takes up only five minutes and is an important form of journaling that makes it easier to become emotionally detached.

It works very well because the first step toward any type of self-improvement is awareness of the problem.

When you're aware of your emotions, you'll be able to pinpoint where you can improve. The more quickly you become aware of how you feel, the more easily you can get back on track. Over time, you'll be able to get better at the way you react to things and you'll be able to be more emotionally consistent.

Do this every night before you go to bed, and you'll be pleasantly surprised at how you'll be able to stay more emotionally consistent.

I want you to recap your day and list these things:

What are three wins you had today?

Just writing this down will help you because it'll make you feel better. We tend to be our biggest critics and beat ourselves down and forget the things we accomplish.

What are three areas you need to get better in?

This alerts you to things you need to improve on.
Also, ask yourself:

What was your highest high?

What was your lowest low?

These two questions make you aware of what made you happiest and what has frustrated you the most.

If you write the same thing down over and over again each night, you'll know what you need to work on in your life and your business.

If you keep writing that your lowest low was "the prospect said 'no' to me," then you've successfully noticed those emotions, and, the next time you're in that moment, you'll be able to react better. Awareness allows you to react in a better way the next time you come across the same situation, and many studies have been done showing how awareness improves your emotional stability (Akshar, Entrepreneur.com, 2020).

If you write the same things down over and over, you'll also be frustrated and may even be angry at yourself. That might push you to make changes so that you won't be writing down the same thing again the next night. (I know that worked well for me.)

The last two questions I want you to answer are:

***What was your best emotion of the day?* (What cheered you up?)**

***What was your worst emotion of the day?* (What got you down?)**

Your best emotion could be your love for your family or your excitement after you made a sale, while your worst emotion could be when you got angry and yelled at your kids.

In summary, I want you to answer the following six questions of the Daily EQ Quiz every night.

1. *What are three wins you had today?*
2. *What are three areas you need to get better in?*
3. *What was your highest high?*
4. *What was your lowest low?*
5. *What was your best emotion of the day?*
6. *What was your worst emotion of the day?* (What got you down?)

Write your answers down in a book or journal or on your phone. I write mine on my phone's Notes app every night, and I find it helpful to go back once in a while to see how I've grown.

The more you do the Daily EQ Quiz, the more you'll become aware of how you're Reacting. This allows you to make a conscious effort to improve yourself.

Remember the *Experience Formula* and how we can't change what happens to us?

Experience = Event + Reaction

We can only control our **Reaction,** and this awareness will make you React better in all situations.

As you React better, your entire experience, all the ups and downs that happen to you, will change for the better. You'll also be able to build your business in spite of fear.

Emotional Consistency Leads to Consistent Actions

In the last few chapters, I've shared tools such as the *Experience Formula*, the *Rejection Killer,* and your *Daily EQ Quiz* to help you become emotionally consistent.

It's so important that you implement these. If you're not consistent with your emotions, you'll never be successful, but if you are, then that emotional consistency will lead to consistent actions.

All businesses have systems, and our next step is to use the *Consistency System* to help you take daily action and reach your goals.

CHAPTER 10

The Consistency System

When I first began my business, I had my big goals written down because I heard leaders teach that having goals was important. I did everything they told me, including setting S.M.A.R.T. goals, which, again, meant my goals were *specific, measurable, achievable, realistic,* and *timely*.

And yet, I struggled with consistency and never reached my goals.

I also heard that having a *big why* was important and that, if your *why* was big enough, you'd make it happen.

That didn't work for me either.

The problem isn't that setting goals doesn't work.

Setting goals works, but it only works if you have the *Consistency System* in place to make sure you take the necessary action.

For every *new* goal you set, you need the *Consistency System* behind the goal to support it; otherwise, you'll never have the time to take the consistent action to achieve that goal.

I don't want you to get discouraged or think something is wrong with you if you get distracted and struggle to stay focused. You're human, and it's harder than ever to stay disciplined because we live in the distraction economy.

Companies like Apple, Samsung, Google, Facebook, TikTok, etc. literally make money when they distract us and make us spend more time using our devices. They profit off of us because the more time we're focused on their devices and platforms, the more ads they can show us and the higher the prices they can charge for those ads.

There are also two laws you have to deal with.

The first is Parkinson's Law, which states that "work expands so as to fill the time available for its completion," so you never get any extra or "free" time to do the things you need to do.

Aristotle also stated that "nature abhors a vacuum," which simply means that things will never be empty because there will always be something that goes into that space.

An example is an empty closet when you first move into your house. Even if you plan to keep it empty, things will naturally pile up and end up inside the closet.

Another example is your daily and weekly schedule. You'll never have the time for your business unless you intentionally set a time to work on your income-producing activities.

I'm sure you've had days where you thought you had some time during the weekend for something, but before you knew it, things came up and you didn't have time to do anything.

I want you to remember this.

You'll *never* have time to work on your goals because something will always come up.

You must *create* the time.

For every new goal you set, you must have the *Consistency System* set up or else you'll never reach that goal.

Even if they didn't consciously create it or aren't aware of it, successful people all have a *Consistency System* in place that makes them take consistent action for maximum achievement.

The Seven Components of the *Consistency System*

There are seven components to the *Consistency System,* and you need to have every one of them in place if you want to achieve a goal.

Component 1: Checklist

You must know exactly what you need to do in order to accomplish your goal.

Component 2: Create and Schedule the Time

How will you have the time to work on the checklist? When will you take action each day? Ideally, you should schedule the same time each day.

Component 3: Determine the Strategy

How will you work on each step of the checklist?

Component 4: Choose Your Environment

Where will you take action?

Component 5: Tracking

How will you measure your progress and know if you're on track?

Component 6: Your Consistency Toolbox

What tools will you be using that'll help you be more efficient with your action steps?

Component 7: Accountability

Who is going to make sure you stay focused and consistent?

Turning My Part-Time Business into a Full-Time Venture

I used the *Consistency System* to support my goal to earn at least $1,000 a week in my home-based business.

Here is what I did to achieve my dream of turning my part-time business into a full-time career.

Component 1: Checklist

I had to reach out to an exact number of new prospects and make a specific number of new sales presentations and follow-ups each day. I also had a calendar of content that I had to publish.

Component 2: Create and Schedule the Time

4:30 p.m. to 5 p.m. from Monday to Friday was blocked out so that I could focus on the checklist. I also set aside 15–30 minutes during my lunch break, and worked another 30 minutes after dinner. I also scheduled two hours on Saturday mornings from 9 a.m. to 11 a.m.

Component 3: Determine the Strategy

Because I had limited time on weekdays, I would batch my sales activities and would only make initial sales approaches during this time. I would do follow-up emails and text messages in the late evenings. Weekends were used for follow-up with old prospects and for planning the following week.

Component 4: Choose Your Environment

I did this in the foyer in my tiny apartment. As I became more confident, I was able to invest 15 more minutes during my lunch break at work and would make calls from my car.

Component 5: Tracking

I used a spreadsheet to track every new person I reached out to and how many sales I made.

Component 6: Your Consistency Toolbox

My tools were my cell phone, computer, instant messaging, text messaging, and teleconferences (this was before smartphones and webinars).

Component 7: Accountability

My mentor would check in with me at least twice a day.

You Are Already Consistent in Some Areas of Your Life

Don't get down on yourself if you haven't been consistent before. You can do it!

I know you can because you're already consistent in some areas of your life, and in each of those activities, you have the *Consistency System* in place.

Here's an example. I know you definitely brush your teeth every day!

Believe it or not, you have the *Consistency System* behind something as simple as brushing your teeth. Let's see how it works.

Component 1: Checklist

You know what you have to do, from squeezing the toothpaste to putting it on the toothbrush.

Component 2: Create and Schedule the Time

You have created a specific time to brush your teeth. It's probably first thing in the morning and last thing before you go to bed.

Component 3: Determine the Strategy

You may start at the bottom and work your way to the top or vice versa, or you may brush the outsides first before the insides. You also may floss before or after brushing.

Component 4: Choose Your Environment

You're most likely brushing in the bathroom.

Component 5: Tracking

Most electric toothbrushes have timers that go off to make sure you brush for at least two minutes. If you're teaching kids the importance of brushing, you may be giving them stickers for every time they brush.

Component 6: Your Consistency Toolbox

Toothbrush, toothpaste, cup, water, floss.

Component 7: Accountability

Your dentist holds you accountable to make sure you're brushing! If you have kids, you also hold them accountable to make sure they brush before going to bed.

You can also apply the *Consistency System* to other things that you do consistently each day, such as taking a shower, cooking dinner for the family, exercising, etc.

In fact, for everything that you do consistently, whether you do it *intentionally* or not, you're using the *Consistency System*.

You need the *Consistency System* to achieve each one of your goals, and I'll help you do that in the next chapter, as I share an embarrassing lesson and a great learning moment of my own.

CHAPTER 11

The Forgotten Soy Sauce

A few years ago, my wife was getting ready to cook and realized we didn't have enough soy sauce. She had me go to Costco to pick up Kikkoman low sodium soy sauce. I could get that anywhere, but Costco sells the huge jug that is much cheaper than buying the small bottles at the grocery store.

I walked in and saw tons of great deals and cool gadgets, so I grabbed a few things, as well as some other goodies that we could make for dinner that week.

I spent over $300 and I was excited to go home and show my wife.

She looked through the three boxes of stuff, and then got really annoyed.

I had gotten so distracted at Costco that I had forgotten to get the soy sauce!

You're probably laughing at me because you know that it's important to have a checklist when you go shopping—especially at Costco!

If you go there without a checklist, you end up buying all kinds of things you didn't intend to buy and can forget the one thing you really needed!

Chances are that you use a checklist for anything you do well, such as running errands, buying groceries, or following an exercise program, so I want you to use a checklist for your business as well.

Writing things down makes them less overwhelming and less stressful.

These checklists keep you focused and on track. They also simplify things because you don't really need to do that many things to be successful. There are only a few activities you have to do each day, and you'll be able to see them very clearly.

Unfortunately, many new entrepreneurs don't use a checklist, and that's why they don't stay consistent and struggle. They act the way I acted at Costco. They're busy doing many things, but often forget the most important thing, and that's why having a checklist is the first component of the *Consistency System*.

For every new goal you set, you must have a checklist that makes it very clear what the exact activity is that you need to do each day, or else you will lose focus.

It's so easy to get distracted today, and that's not your fault. I mentioned in the last chapter that we live in the distraction economy, where companies make money by trying to get us to spend as much time as possible on their platforms.

We live in an age where we can listen to any song, watch any movie, or buy anything online within seconds. It's the age of instant gratification and endless temptations, and it's hard to avoid these distractions and stay consistent.

This is the same reason I struggled in the beginning. I did "something" and thought I was working on my business, but I didn't do the most important income-producing activities.

I was approaching my business the hard way. I didn't have a checklist, I didn't have anyone to help me stay consistent, and I was wasting my time on endless trainings.

One of the turning points for me was when I created my checklist called *The DMO (Daily Method of Operation)* that helped me become one of the top sales recruiters in my company for five straight years.

Be on Offense Instead of Defense

Checklists allow you to be on the offense instead of playing defense and catch-up.

Instead of waking up and reacting to emails or messages from people asking you to do things, you go out and attack the most important thing you have to do for the day.

Top leaders always work on their checklists first because that's the only way they can achieve their goals on time. This doesn't need to take up much time, but you need to set aside at least 15 minutes before you tackle any of the other things in life that don't move you toward your goal.

Focus on Activity and Not Results

A mistake that many new entrepreneurs make is that they do their checklist for a few days and then quit because of the lack of results.

Results take time.

You have to be patient. I know that, if you're reading this, you're not into "get rich quick" schemes!

You have to give it time for you to get good.

If you focus on just doing your checklist every day for 30 days, you'll see massive changes in yourself and discover it's not only doable, but it gives you tremendous satisfaction and happiness.

You'll feel fulfilled because you're finally taking the actions that move you toward achieving your goal.

And before you know it, the happiness and success will compound exponentially because you'll be getting the results that you wanted.

Be patient with yourself and make sure you don't quit in the first week.

Scale Your Business by Increasing Your Team's Productivity

Let's suppose you woke up your sales team in the middle of the night and you asked them, "What are the five things you must do each day to build your business?" What would they say?

If they can't answer that simple question, then you need to start having your team use checklists ASAP! Systems are crucial for business, and a checklist is the foundation of any system.

Not only does a checklist help you stay focused and on track, but it'll help you scale and grow your team as your business grows.

Why?

It's because people have been programmed and trained since birth to follow checklists and to-do lists.

In school, we're taught to complete assignments (a checklist of projects).

At jobs, we're taught to work on specific projects (another checklist).

**Most people are not productive if they
don't have a checklist to follow.**

If we don't know exactly what we need to do, then we will struggle and our business output will drop.

Many entrepreneurs preach a lot about vision, but the problem is that most people don't know anything about vision.

Before I became an entrepreneur, the only "vision" I knew was that I had LASIK eye surgery and had 20/10 vision!

Vision is hard to teach and is a difficult concept to understand, but a checklist is easy to follow.

If you want your team to take the action that'll grow your business fast, they need to have a checklist and follow it daily.

A checklist helps your team to:

- Stay focused
- Create consistency
- Get more done in less time
- Avoid info overwhelm
- Grow your business exponentially

If your business doesn't already have a checklist, I suggest you start out with *The DMO (Daily Method of Operation)* checklist that I used to become a top sales recruiter.

The DMO 3-5-5-5-3 Checklist for Home-Based Businesses

The DMO is a simple business checklist. It's focused entirely on sales activities because every new business needs new sales.

For home-based businesses, over 90% of your time needs to be spent on sales until you reach your first $100,000 a year in gross sales. For traditional businesses, the number is $1 million a year.

Most new entrepreneurs start out focused on sales and then make the mistake of spending more time managing and creating systems instead of selling.

> *Without systems or good management, a home-based business won't grow, but it can still survive if it has new sales coming in.*

However, the opposite is *not* true.

Without new sales, no business can survive! No systems can save a business if it doesn't have new sales coming in, and that's why *The DMO* checklist is focused on income-generating activities.

If your home-based business is already making over $100,000 a year, then you have to make sure your new team and sales staff is focused on *The DMO*.

Here's *The DMO's* 3-5-5-5-3 checklist and what each number stands for.

3 → Post Three Pieces of Content on Social Media

People are watching you on social media.

This activity refers to three different types of posts. The easiest way to do this is to post once on your newsfeed (profile) and do two "Stories" posts. These posts should create curiosity about what you do.

5 → Meet Five New Contacts a Day

Without new leads, your sales will dry up. You constantly have to add new people to your sales funnel. Social media has made it easy to meet new contacts. Treat this as "you have to meet five new friends a day."

5 → Invite Five People to See if They're Interested

Once you have new contacts, then you have to approach a minimum of five people a day to see if they're open to learning about what you have to offer. Most will say "*no,*" and that's okay. Your goal is to simply let them know what you have to offer.

5 → Follow Up with Five Prospects

Most people will not buy right away, so the fortune is in the follow-up. Every person will eventually buy, join, or give you a referral, but you must stay consistent with your follow-ups.

The old rule that 80% of sales are made after the fifth follow-up still applies today.

3 → Send a Sales Presentation to Three People

A minimum of three people have to watch a sales presentation every day. Making this happen can be as easy as sending them an online video, inviting them to attend a webinar, giving a one-on-one in-person presentation, or inviting someone to a group presentation at a hotel.

These numbers are the *bare* minimum and are something everyone can achieve.

If you don't hit these numbers every day, you'll be out of business pretty quickly.

The DMO is also important if you've had some success already. It makes you focus on sales instead of being distracted and makes you go into management mode. Your business will never grow itself until you hit a critical mass, and until then, you must keep on bringing in new sales.

If you have a home-based business, remember that 90% of your time should be spent generating new sales until you reach $100,000 a year. If you have a traditional business, you should be focusing on sales until you reach your first million.

If You Don't Have Time to Work on a Checklist

When you see a checklist like *The DMO,* you may say that you don't have the time to do everything on the list.

But you do have the time!

Even though you only have the same 24 hours in a day as everyone else, in the next chapter, I'm going to teach you how to *create* the time. You'll also discover strategies to help you to stick to a schedule that'll help you get any checklist done.

CHAPTER 12

Create the Time

It's easy to set goals. We get excited and write down huge lists of things we want to accomplish.

As entrepreneurs, we have unlimited ambitions but limited time. We still only have 24 hours in each day. We don't get an extra 25th hour or even an extra minute to do what needs to be done.

That's why Component 2 of the *Consistency System* is to **Create and Schedule the Time** to work on your checklist of things to do.

Life is full of nonstop distractions, so that's why you have to strategically plan, schedule, and create the time, or else you'll never have the time to make your goals become reality.

Schedules allow you to focused on what needs to be done before the distractions get to you.

Instead of waking up and reacting to emails or messages, you have to go out and attack the most important thing for the day. And that is your checklist!

I've interviewed more than 700 top business leaders on my podcast and they all say they work on their checklists first because they know that their checklists are what's going to determine whether they hit their goals.

You need to set aside 15 minutes in the morning to focus on things that move you toward your goals before you tackle the other things in life that don't help your business.

But how do you get those extra 15 minutes?

Say "No" to Something You're Currently Doing

We still *only have 24 hours in a day.* More time won't magically appear. So how do you work on the checklist with the same 86,400 seconds?

This is not like working on a project where you can ask for more money and a bigger budget. There is no extra time!

So, what can you do?

You "create" that time by learning to say "no."

The most important word that an entrepreneur must learn to say is "*no.*" To get the time you need, you must say "no" more often than before.

If you need to commit to working on your checklist, where will you get that time?

You must either do *less* of what you're currently doing or stop doing something altogether.

- You may have to sleep less (which I don't recommend).
- You may have to stop working on a project that you're involved in.
- You may have to spend less time on eating lunch and take a shorter lunch break.
- You may have to give up relaxation and leisure time, like watching TV.
- You should probably stop wasting time trying to sell to bad prospects.

If you don't have the discipline to say "*no,*" you'll never have the time to focus on the checklist that'll help you achieve your goal.

Work in Small Chunks of Time

When you first create the checklist of things you have to do to accomplish your goal (Component 1), you may feel overwhelmed and say you don't have the time to do all this.

But you do have the time.

Many of the items on your checklist can be done in small chunks of time, especially if they relate to selling.

You don't need hours. You just need short bursts of 15 minutes of focus where you're not multitasking.

In our *Purpose Driven Networkers* community, we prospect together two times a day in short 15-minute sessions and another 15-minute replay that members can access anytime.

New members usually have some difficulty getting their checklists done, but it gets easier and easier as they learn to overcome their fears and overthinking.

By the third week, most members can get this entire sales checklist done in less than 45 minutes a day.

I understand that you may not be able to do everything in one sitting.

Between work and family commitments, most part-time entrepreneurs don't even have *one hour* to focus entirely on sales activities, but you can do them in the little nooks and crannies of your day.

Here are some ideas for you to get your checklist done.

You can reach out and text three prospects on your five-minute coffee break at work.

You can spend 20 minutes of your lunch break meeting some new friends on Facebook, Instagram, TikTok, or LinkedIn.

You can follow up with three to five prospects as you sit in your car waiting to pick up your kids from school.

Thanks to technology and social media, you don't need to be at a desk. You can work your business on your phone and on the go.

Go "Watch a TV Episode!"

Watching TV is one of the biggest wastes of time out there, so I'm not telling you to actually watch TV! However, this tip will help change the way you think and increase your productivity.

Sometimes you may have a task on your checklist that requires a longer period of time to accomplish, such as preparing a budget, working on a new sales presentation, putting together a training for your team, etc.

These tasks will require more than 15 minutes of focused time, but most people make two specific mistakes.

First, they waste their time by multitasking.

Tons of studies have been done that show that multitasking decreases your productivity and that you'll just never get your checklist completed if you multitask (Quast, 2017). You worked hard to say "*no*" to things to create this time, so don't waste it by multitasking!

The second mistake is not realizing that we have limited willpower and focus. Very few people can focus and work on a single task at maximum productivity for more than 52 minutes at a time (Businessinsider. com, 2016).

After 52 minutes, your brain gets tired, you lose focus, and you don't do good work anymore. There is a point of diminishing return where the more you work at something, the worse you get. There is no point in continuing.

If you can't work well, there is no point in continuing to keep going! You should take a five-to-10-minute break and get back to your other responsibilities.

There is a myth and perception that entrepreneurs can grind and work on one thing for an entire day. That is more of a fairy-tale than fact. Most achievements are done in consistent short bursts of focused time where the person is working at maximum productivity. In fact, you work best in short bursts, 30-minute blocks of time where you work for 25 minutes and then take a five-minute break (Lifehacker, 2019).

You can work on something for a longer time, but it's just not going to be productive. Your time might as well be spent on something else.

It's also not very motivating if you know you have to work on something for hours. You either feel like you don't have time or it sounds long and boring.

Instead, say to yourself, *I'm going to watch a TV episode* because everyone has the ability to focus for just 30 minutes.

When I plan out my day, I look at my calendar and ask myself, *When can I watch a quick episode?* and that's the time when I set aside 30 minutes to focus on my checklist.

Schedule a Set Time Every Day

Once you've said "no" to things and created your time, you need to do your best to choose the *same time every day* to work on the checklist.

It should be the same time because we do things consistently that way.

Think of activities such as brushing your teeth, taking a shower, cooking dinner, etc. You do all those things consistently, and I'm sure you do them at around the same time each day.

Do you exercise consistently? If you do, you probably exercise at a set time each day and you stick to that schedule. If you struggle to exercise consistently, one of the main reasons is because you don't have a set schedule.

You don't need much time to work on the checklist, but you must schedule doing it at the same time each day into your calendar. You can start small and just schedule 15 minutes, or "*Go watch a TV episode*" and give yourself 30 minutes.

Remember that how often you work on your checklist is more important than how long you do it for, so schedule that time into your calendar.

It should always be the same time every day, and one of those times should be early in the morning.

The best time to work on your checklist is first thing in the morning, before life and other work responsibilities distract you and suck away your mental energy.

New Entrepreneurs Need to Treat Their Business Like a Job

Have you ever planned to make time to work on something important but found yourself distracted and not sticking to that commitment you made to yourself?

This was one of my biggest lightbulb moments as a new entrepreneur.

I was struggling with consistency in early 2004 and wasn't working on my checklist every day. Some days I would do it, and other days I would slack off and skip it. As a result, I wasn't making money in my part-time business, and I was stuck at a job that I hated.

One afternoon I was really annoyed at my boss for making me show up for a lunch meeting in Koreatown in Los Angeles. It was at a nice restaurant with great food, but I had to go through terrible Friday afternoon Los Angeles traffic. It was at an awful time of the day on the worst day of the week to be driving.

Halfway into the meeting, I realized I didn't even really need to be there. I was really irritated, but the damage had been done.

The meeting had ruined my plans for that evening because it prevented me from getting my work done and made me have to stay late at work. I was really angry that I had to go, but I had shown up anyway because my boss told me to.

And then it hit me how stupid I was!

I realized that I was showing up for something that I didn't want to do and that had *no* benefit for my future wealth. And yet I would not show up to work on my own business checklist every day.

I decided at that very second that I would show up every day for myself!

If I had to skip something, I would skip a meeting with my boss before I skipped working on my checklist. I knew that I should *never* skip the time I set to work on my checklist. If I did, I'd never achieve my goal of making enough money in my part-time business that I could leave that dreadful job.

I started to treat my part-time business like a job, and that is exactly the same thing I want you to do.

You must show up for the activities on your checklist as if your boss told you to do so!

Schedule your checklist of activities onto your calendar. Shut off distractions and don't multitask. It's the same as if you were meeting with your boss—only in this case, you are your own boss.

Still Don't Have Enough Time?

Your schedule is packed already, so how will you create the time to work on your checklist?

Time management is a common problem for most people, but you do have the time if you follow these *10 Rules of the Consistency Productivity Regimen* that you're about to learn.

CHAPTER 13

10 Rules of the Consistency Productivity Regimen

One of the obstacles to consistency is the perceived "lack" of time. Everyone says they're "busy" or they "don't have time," but the reality is that you do have time.

People know that "time is money," but not many people actually treat time as real cash!

Time is your most precious asset and the only thing you can't get back. You can get money back and, in some cases, thanks to modern medicine and proper nutrition, you can even get parts of your health back. But time is the one thing you can never get back.

Here are the *10 Rules of the Consistency Productivity Regimen* that will help you get more done in less time. If you follow these rules, you'll be happy and fulfilled because you'll feel that you've created an extra two hours in your life.

If you ignore these rules, then you'll never have the time to work on your checklist and take the consistent action to be successful.

Rule 1: Be a Defender of Your Time

Success begins in the mind, and having a productive day is the same way.

You must make a conscious decision to battle against the nonstop distractions and win the day.

You can't just wake up and have a carefree approach. If you do that, you'll be sucked in to different things and end up not achieving anything you want to accomplish.

You must take a firm stand and decide every morning that *you'll do everything to battle against the forces of distraction and stay focused.*

We're human and can be tempted easily. Without this mental determination, you have no chance of winning against the distractions that life throws at you.

Rule 2: 95% of Time Management Is Attitude

Most people think it's the tricks and things you do that create more time, but it's all about your attitude and how you perceive things.

You know how you don't have time to follow up with 10 people?

If someone told you that they'd brutally attack your loved ones if you didn't follow up, you'd magically find the time to do it!

That's an extreme and unpleasant example. Of course, no one will ever brutally attack your loved ones, and that's why you find excuses to say you don't have time.

There are other examples that are less severe. If your boss told you that you would get a 5% decrease in pay if you didn't make those follow-up calls, then you'd magically find the time to make them.

If the consequences are severe, you'll always find the time to make something happen, and that makes you realize that, in the end, it's all about excuses.

Rule 3: Plan Your Week

"H.K. Williams once said, "If you fail to prepare, you are preparing to fail."

(https://quoteinvestigator.com/2018/07/08/plan/)

All top achievers plan out their days, weeks, and some even their years.

Tom Brady, arguably the greatest NFL quarterback of all time, micromanages every activity in his days. He has every workout, practice, treatment, meal, and rest time all scheduled three years in advance (www. SI.com, 2014).

The best time to plan your week is on weekends and before the new work week starts. My favorite day to recap and plan is on Sundays.

Here's how to plan your week. It should take you no more than five to 10 minutes.

Step 1: Make a list of things you'd like to accomplish this week.

Step 2: Choose the *three most important* things from Step 1 and then cross out the rest.

One of the three things *must* be one of your income-producing activities for your business!

Why only three things?

It's because you have limited time and, outside of your job and normal responsibilities, such as running errands, parenting, school, attending business training events, etc., you really do *not* have that much time.

Another reason is that you'll get better results if you're laser-focused on just the three most important tasks.

Success is about doing a few things really well instead of doing many things less well.

Step 3: Rank the Three Items in Order of Priority

Here's an example:

#1: Spend an hour each day on prospecting and approach 20 people you have never before shared your business with.

#2: Update your Facebook profile picture.

#3: Attend weekly team training call.

Step 4: Schedule the Top Three Tasks into Your Calendar

You must create the time, so you need to *block off* the time to work on the checklist or else it'll never happen, because you're going to be bombarded with endless distractions.

These time blocks are for you to prospect and nothing else!

Never sacrifice working on the checklist for admin work that can wait until later. Personal development is also important, but that's best done during "down time"—you can listen to a podcast while you're driving or exercising. Personal development should never take the place of working on your checklist.

My favorite tool for planning is Google Calendar, and I have it synced with my phone, tablets, and computers.

Once you have scheduled your checklist items into your calendar, treat that "meeting with yourself" as you would a meeting with someone else.

Just like you would show up to a meeting with someone else, you must show up for yourself and your fortune-building time. Treat it like a job!

If you're running a part-time business from home, you may not get a huge block of time in the day to focus exclusively on your business. As you learned in the last chapter, you can split the time into small 15 minutes blocks of time or "go watch a TV episode" and schedule 30 minutes.

The best way to make sure you show up is by scheduling time to work on your business at the same time each day. Create that routine.

Rule 4: Plan Your Day the Night Before

Every night, before you go to bed, you're going to do the same thing as we just did for the week, but this time you're going to do it for the following day.

Choose the three most important things you must do, rank them, and then schedule them into your calendar.

Ideally you don't need to schedule your time for your business because you already did that when you planned your week.

Rule 5: Plan Out Your Prospects

Most new entrepreneurs waste mental energy and the small amount of time they have on deciding *who* they should reach out to.

They finally have the time to work on their businesses, but waste it by scrolling on their newsfeeds or filtering messages to find people to reach out to, and then time runs out.

Every second of your time should be spent on sales-generating activities on your checklist.

To increase your productivity, spend time on the weekends and especially the night before to *plan* out your prospects. You have to be intentional! Here are some ideas for what you could do:

1. Go to my biking group on Facebook and meet five new friends.
2. Follow up with five college friends who I haven't talked to in months (Terrence, Kevin, Bob, Kathy, Joe).
3. Follow up with five prospects who I reached out to earlier this year (Joe, Mary, Jane, Harvey, Scott).
4. Approach three of my neighbors and see if they want to be customers (Victor, Tim, Stacy).

Be *intentional* and start each day knowing exactly what you have to do—otherwise, you're going to waste tons of time and never get anything productive done.

Rule 6: Always Have an End Time to Every Task

As you schedule your tasks, always set an end time where the activity must stop. This prevents things from taking too long and ruining the rest of your planned day.

Use a timer and, once the time is over, you must move to the next task on the calendar.

This creates urgency, making you stay focused and work faster. It also decreases the chance of you wasting time with overthinking and the endless drive for perfection.

If you find yourself not able to finish what you have to do in a time block, you have planned too many things! In that case, you need to focus on doing less and also push yourself to go quicker during the time you have!

I find it best to schedule things in 15- and 30-minute chunks of time, because it gets harder to focus in any span longer than that.

Again, once the timer is up, you *must* move on to the next step.

Everything should have an end time, including phone calls. Never let a phone call last forever. Once you get on a call, let the person know you have only 15 minutes to talk because you have another meeting coming up.

Rule 7: Two-Second Rule

The Two-Second Rule prevents overthinking and gets you to take action fast. It has helped many people I've coached to overcome fear.

Here is how it works.

The moment you think of someone you "should reach out to," you need to reach out to that person ASAP—in under two seconds.

That is really easy to do with smartphones today. You just need to take your phone out and send that person a message.

By taking fast action, you prevent yourself from talking yourself out of it.

If you're in a situation where you really can't reach out to a person immediately, then write it down and do it the first chance you get. When you think of someone while you're driving, you can simply leave an audio message on your phone's notepad to remind yourself. Once you reach your destination and park your car, immediately send that person a message.

Rule 8: Avoid Multitasking

By now, you've read more than a few times that you should stop multitasking, and you're going to learn why.

Our brains work better and become more efficient when we're doing the same type of activity over and over again. Every time we start a new thing, it takes our brains a few minutes to warm up and adjust.

A good example is exercising and reading. It's much easier to exercise for 30 minutes than it is to exercise for five minutes and then read for five minutes, and then go back to exercising, and to keep doing this back and forth! You won't have a good workout and you won't remember what you read.

Here's a common mistake that many new entrepreneurs make. They want to create a good social media post, but, while they're in the middle of writing the post, they reply back to someone who messages them. When they go back to finishing their post, they've lost their train of thought and have to take minutes to read and think back to what they were going to post.

Another example is when you're replying to someone's message, but then all of a sudden you get a notification that someone commented on your social media post. You look at that notification and then, when you go back to your message, you have to reread what you wrote and spend a few seconds to remember what you were going to say.

In both examples, you've wasted 20–30 seconds or sometimes even minutes on getting your thoughts back, and *that is time you'll never get back in your life.*

You would have done much better if you had focused on what you were doing first and then paid attention to the second task later.

This happens to most people throughout the day—so it's no wonder people don't have time!

If you're still not convinced that multitasking kills productivity and makes you "dumber," here's a simple and fun game to prove it.

I want you to count from 1 to 10 as quickly as possible, like this.

1, 2, 3, 4, 5, etc.

Do it now. It should take you less than two seconds. Ready, set, go!

Now I want you to say the first 10 letters of the alphabet as fast as possible, like this.

A, B, C, D, E, etc.

Do that now.

That should have taken you one to two seconds.

Now try this. Combine what we just did and say the first number and then the first letter, like this.

1A, 2B, 3C, etc.

And do that as fast as possible!

I'm sure it took you way longer to combine the number and letter than it did to say them separately!

You see?! Multitasking slows you down and makes you "dumber"!

Rule 9: Batching

Instead of multitasking, learn to batch tasks. Do the same **type of activity** at the same time. Our brains have to "warm up" and get used to every new activity. This is a reason why multitasking doesn't work.

You probably do this all the time already. You run all your errands at once. You don't run one errand and go home and then go back to run another errand and go home.

If you have follow-up messages to reply to, set asides 10 minutes to send out all the follow-up messages before you send out other types of reach outs. Don't jump back and forth between different types of activities.

You get much more done when you focus on one type of task at a time.

Rule 10: Learn to Say "No" More Often

In the last chapter, you learned how you have to say "no" and stop doing some things you're currently doing so that you can create the time to work on your checklist.

You also must say "no" to new opportunities and distractions that come up. Stop looking at shiny new objects!

You have limited time and energy, and everything you pay attention to sucks it up. It's like your phone battery. Everything you do drains it little by little.

If people approach you to look at different things, say "no!"

Not "maybe" or "send me the info and I'll take a look at it." Just say "no!"

Saying "no" will let you focus on your business and will give you the freedom you want.

You can say "no" in a friendly manner. This is what I say all the time.

> *"Thanks for thinking of me. Right now, I'm working on a major project and I need to focus on it. But please check back with me six months from now. Thanks for your understanding."*

This script is also a test to see if the person is wasting my time. If I don't get a follow-up in six months, that means I've saved myself valuable time. It means that the person is not successful (because of the lack of follow-up) or that the opportunity was never that good to begin with.

If you want to attract better people in your life, saying "no" will also get their attention. No successful person respects anyone who gives away their time so easily.

Taking the First Step Doesn't Need to Be That Hard

Now that you know the importance of having a checklist and how to create the time to work on it, how do you actually start taking action?

Taking the first step is often the hardest part of the process, but there are many tricks and strategies that help you overcome fear and allow you to start getting results, fast.

CHAPTER 14

The Game Plan

Just like a plane uses the most fuel during takeoff, getting started on your business checklist is often the hardest part of working towards a goal.

We all have fears that hold us back, and Component 3 of the *Consistency System* is **having a strategy** to get you to take action ASAP.

It doesn't matter what tactical strategies you plan to implement, such as online advertising, content creation, networking in specific groups, etc. **The most important strategy is the exact steps that will help you take action ASAP** before you get distracted and lose the motivation.

Make It Easy

Many new entrepreneurs make the mistake of starting out by tackling the big project, going after the big sale, and trying to hit a home run on their first at bat.

These big tasks are often scary. They also make you strive for perfection, which causes procrastination.

You need momentum, and you create that momentum by taking small, easy action steps.

You need to determine the easiest thing on your checklist and work on that first. It should be easy to get this task done, which leads to fulfillment and increases your confidence.

This creates the momentum so that you'll eventually be able to work on the bigger projects.

Never forget that *consistency beats intensity!*

Make It Simple

Another mistake is setting up complicated systems that take time to learn and adapt.

These systems can be new apps, software, and tools or even just a complicated daily schedule that is hard to follow.

These are all obstacles that distract you from what really matters.

Instead, keep it simple.

If you have a big task you must achieve, then break it down into smaller steps. Small steps make things less intimidating and motivate you to get started.

Make It Quick

Making it easy and simple means you want to start with quick working sessions. As long as you don't multitask, these can be as short as 15-minute time blocks.

If you struggle with being focused on taking action, the worst thing you can do is to go all out and schedule a big chunk of time to work on your checklist.

Many new entrepreneurs go for intensity instead of consistency and then they burn out, especially if they've never done anything intense in their life before.

Intensity also requires a lot of time.

Here's an example:

If you've never spent more than an hour a day on your part-time business, and then decide that you're going to go for a 90-day challenge, you're setting yourself up for failure.

The first obstacle is time. Where are you going to find the extra 60–120 minutes every day to go for this blitz?

How you will have the mental stamina?

It's like if someone who has never worked out decides to go to the gym for an hour a day for seven straight days.

They're going to be super sore and will hurt so badly after the first day that they'll never want to go back.

I see this happen to many new entrepreneurs who try to build businesses while still having full-time jobs.

They struggle with consistency because they set unrealistic expectations like spending three hours a day on their businesses when they've never even worked on them for 15 minutes a day for three straight days before.

I want you to remember that *consistency beats intensity!*

Don't get frustrated if you don't have the stamina or focus to work an hour on your business. You can start small and slowly build up.

Remember, it's not the amount of time you spend on your business that's important, but how often you work on your checklist.

It's how often you show up that will make you a winner!

Three Rules to Follow

Here are three simple rules that I learned from New York Times bestselling author James Clear that will get you going fast, especially if you're struggling with being consistent in sales.

Rule 1: Start with *one* when it comes to prospecting. That can mean doing just *one* sales call today. Just one. You're not allowed to do more than one the first day.

In our *Purpose Driven Networkers* community, we have a mantra, *"One is better than none!"*

Even on days when you're tired and burned out, remember that *"One is better than none!"* and send out one sales message a day.

Rule 2: Add one each day. If you started with one call today, then do two sales calls tomorrow. And then do three the following day and so on.

Rule 3: Once you reach a big enough number that you either don't have the time or stamina to go on, then break that up into two parts.

Here's an example.

You get to 20 sales calls and you don't have the mental stamina to continue or you just don't have the time to do it.

At this point, instead of stopping or cutting back, you're going to divide 20 sales calls into two blocks of 10 calls. From then on, start with two segments of 10 sales calls each and do these during different parts of the day.

You can do 10 first thing in the morning and another 10 during lunch time.

Then apply Rule 1 to these two segments again, but this time start with 10 and add one each day to get 11 calls per time block and so on. You simply repeat these three rules.

These three rules work really well to help you start small and create consistency.

Now that you know how to get started working toward a goal, let's look at how to keep going even if you get burned out and tired.

CHAPTER 15

Surroundings for Success

Your surroundings play a big part in your success. Component 4 of the *Consistency System* is that you must *Choose Your Environment*.

Your environment is a mental trigger that can either help you or hurt you.

Just like a recovering alcoholic will not be able to stay sober if he hangs out with friends at a bar overnight, you won't be able to take consistent action toward your goals if you're in the wrong environment.

There are different elements to creating a winning environment. I'm going to share three tips with you that will get you in the mood to do the things on your checklist every day.

1. Change the People
2. Use a Unique Location
3. Play the Same Song

Change the People

My mentor, the late business philosopher Jim Rohn, once said, "You're the average of the five people you spend the most time with."

The people around you will either lift you up or bring you down.

Always ask yourself, *Are the people I spend time with helping me advance toward my goals?*

If they're not, you need to slowly distance yourself from those people and meet new friends.

They may be great human beings, but they're not helping you achieve what you want to accomplish. You can solve this by not hanging out with those people. Go meet new friends.

Sometimes the situation is more complicated when the people closest to us (like our families) are the ones who hold us back. In cases like this, you can't change them, but you can decide who you want to surround yourself with, especially when it comes to working on the checklist.

It's nearly impossible to get motivated if the people around you distract you from doing what needs to be done. If you find yourself in this situation, just change your location.

For example, if you feel your spouse is not supportive of what you're doing, you can always go to a different room (or even work in your car) so that you can get your checklist done.

When I was expanding my business into Malaysia, I had to work around the time zone difference. That meant I had to make sales calls at 10 p.m. in Los Angeles.

This was in the early stages of my entrepreneurial career, and my wife and I lived in a tiny one-bedroom apartment. Even though she was very supportive of my business, the last thing she wanted to hear after a long day at her own job was my loud voice on the phone.

I don't blame her, since I knew she wanted to relax and get ready for work the next day, but I knew I couldn't prospect effectively knowing that I was disturbing her. So, I changed my environment and location. I went outside and walked up and down the streets of Santa Monica, making one call after another until it was finally time to go to bed around 1 a.m.

I had another coaching client who was able to build a successful part-time business after work by making calls inside his car. He realized that, once he got home, he never got any of his checklist done because he couldn't resist hanging out with his kids. To change his environment, he would park a block from his house and get a good 15 minutes of sales calls done before he went home to hug his kids.

Use a Unique Location

Those two examples are ways in which you can change who is around you and where you are working. It's a good idea to choose a unique location to work on your checklist and on the business itself.

We tend to lose focus when we stay in the same environment for a long time, and this prevents you from staying consistent and productive (Trello. com, 2018).

This is the reason why most people say they exercise more consistently when they go to a gym rather than exercising in a home gym. It's also a reason why people like to work at coffee shops. The atmosphere inspires them to get to work.

You don't always have to go outside to choose your unique location. You can move to a different place in your home for a short time period.

Here are other examples of ways that I've changed my location that have helped me stay consistent:

I write down ideas for my social media content from my backyard. Seeing nature and hearing the sound of birds makes me more creative.

I recap and plan out my next day when I'm outside walking my dog at night.

I do yoga on my front porch and then read for 15 minutes before I eat breakfast.

Every day, immediately after I exercise, I write down 10 ideas for how to grow my business when I walk around the block to cool down.

Those are just some examples of how you can choose a unique location to help you stay consistent with your checklist.

Play the Same Song

The last part of creating an environment that'll help you achieve your goals is to use music to get you going.

Music is a great emotional trigger that creates feelings and gets you in a certain mood. I'm sure that, if you hear certain songs, they'll bring you back to your childhood, teenage years, your wedding day, etc. (*Bergland*, 2013).

Play the same song every time you work on your checklist, so that when you play that song, it'll get you in the mood to do what you need to do.

It works because your song is "anchored" and it's all part of Neuro-Linguistic Programming (NLP). You don't need to understand the technical side of how it works, but just know that it does!

Playing the same song is a great way to get back into action if you get off track. Just make sure you use that song specifically for that purpose or you'll ruin the anchoring effect.

Here are three examples of how I use music to create myself an environment where I can take consistent action:

1. Every time I work out and lift weights, I play the song "Triumph" by the Wu Tang Clan over and over again. I've done this for years so that every time I listen to that song, it gets me into the mood to lift weights, even on days when I don't feel like it.

2. I've done over 1,000 presentations and spoken on stage on different continents, but I still get nervous before I speak. I listen to AC/DC's "Thunderstruck" right before I'm about to speak, and that fires me up and helps me to take action in spite of that fear.

3. I also played the song "Music to Enhance Intellect & Creativity" by Dr. Mythili thousands of times when I wrote this book. Just hearing that song motivated me to get going and write.

How to Improve Quickly

The late business guru Peter Drucker once famously said, "What gets measured gets improved." By that, he meant that you can't know how well you're doing unless you track what you do.

The next component of the *Consistency System* is about tracking and what you should be doing each day so that you can make quick improvements.

CHAPTER **16**

Get 1% Better Each Day with This Tip

Most people take on new goals without any tracking.

If you don't track or measure, not only will you not know how you're doing, but the process will also become extremely boring and discouraging. It is very hard to stay consistent when you have no idea how close you are to the finish line.

Tracking Creates Consistency

Not only does tracking give you hope, but it also becomes a game that creates consistency.

Jerry Seinfeld, comedian and actor, once shared that what made him consistent was using a simple calendar. Every time he wrote a joke, he put a big "X" on that day. He did this for a few days, and then the next thing you know, he never wanted to end that streak. His whole goal was to write a joke each day so that he could put the big "X" on the calendar (jamesclear.com).

I had one of my coaching clients apply Seinfeld's calendar routine, and, within a few weeks, he went from struggling to being one of the most consistent salespeople I know.

You're about to discover simple ways to track your progress that'll motivate you to take consistent action. If you don't do this, it's extremely easy to quit and stop working on your checklist.

Tracking Your Sales Numbers and Conversion

If you only track one thing in any business, it should be your sales process. It'll reveal how consistent and productive you are.

For example, you can track:

How many people do you need to talk to before they agree to listen to a presentation?

How many presentations do you have to do before someone becomes a customer?

This can be expanded into marketing by tracking things like the number of people who need to see your ad before you get a sale.

Most new salespeople burn out and quit because they don't track their numbers. However, if you know your numbers, it'll help you stay motivated because you'll know that you're getting closer to a result.

This really helped me when I first started.

I had no sales experience, and it took me reaching out to 42 people before I got my first sale. Many people would have quit, but I didn't because my mentor told me that one out of every 100 people I talked to would buy. I listened to his advice and tracked every conversation, getting more optimistic the closer I got to 100. Knowing that I would eventually get a sale as I approached 100 people gave me hope and kept me going.

You may think that one out of 42 is a poor conversion rate, but I actually thought I was pretty good because I did better than the expectation that my mentor had created for me.

When I'm coaching new entrepreneurs struggling in sales, the first question I ask them is how many people they've approached.

When I get answers like "20 or 30," I then ask them what the exact number is. Is it 20 or 30? There is a big difference between 20 and 30!

When I was presenting to my 20th prospect, I couldn't get them to see the value of what I was selling, but when I was talking to my 30th prospect, I could almost get them to buy. But I just couldn't close. Even though I didn't get a sale, I realized through my tracking that I did get better. This gave me hope and encouragement.

Tracking helps you keep going regardless of the outcome. When you track your performance, you'll see your skill set and your numbness to rejection improve very quickly when you do a high number of calls.

I don't want to get into fancy metrics because there are tons of things you can track, but what you track can be as simple as:

1. How many people you've approached
2. How many people watched a sales presentation
3. How many people purchased

To keep it simple, you can start by tracking just those three numbers.

Over time, you'll see yourself get better. Your confidence will increase, as personal growth is very fulfilling.

Track Your Time

Time management is similar to money management. If you want to save money, you have to track how much you spend each month. If you want to succeed at business, you have to track how much time you actually work on your business.

How much time do you actually spend on your checklist?

Many people think they're working on their business when they're actually just wasting time scrolling on their social media newsfeeds, checking random emails and messages, or jumping from one distraction to another.

When you first track your time, you'll be shocked at how much time you're wasting!

Remember Peter Drucker's quote, "What gets measured gets improved." Make sure you track your time!

Take a Consistency Huddle

Another way to track is to take a Consistency Huddle. These are small breaks each day to evaluate how well you're doing and to get you back on track.

In sports such as football, soccer, and basketball, time-outs are called to allow the players to regroup and strategize. Teams also take halftime breaks and go to the locker room to recap, analyze, and make improvements to their game plans.

You must do this as well because your day rarely goes according to plan!

Distractions that drain our mental energy make us go off track, and it's important for you to catch yourself doing the wrong things before it's too late.

Take one to two minutes in the middle of the day and see how much of the stuff you said you were going to do actually *got* done.

If you're like me, you'll discover you've gone off track and maybe done only a few of the things you had planned, but don't get discouraged. It happens to everyone.

What's important is for you to be aware of what's happened and for you to get back on track! Refer back to your checklist and the things you had planned for the day.

I usually take my Consistency Huddle around 12:30 p.m. when I walk my "first son" (my dog, Obi). Just like you, I discover I've only done one or two of the things I had planned out. But here's the next important step.

The second part of this huddle is to *decide* on the very next three action steps to take once the break is over. You do these three things and *nothing else* because this will help you get back on the original plan you had scheduled the night before.

I write down three things I am going to do as soon as I walk into the house and feed Obi.

This means that, once Obi is fed, I get right into action and work on the first item. I don't check social media, check emails, go to the bathroom, etc.

These Consistency Huddles are a super effective way for you to get back on track and have worked so well that I now implement this system throughout my day.

I do this before I nap…before I play baseball with my boys…before I take a bathroom break…

In each Consistency Huddle, I see how I'm doing compared to my original schedule and then write down the three action steps I'm going to take *immediately* after my break is over.

These huddles have helped my coaching clients stay focused, get more done in less time, and stay consistent.

Your Very Next Action Determines Your Success

Remember, it's okay if you get sidetracked, but it's how quickly you become aware and jump right back into action that is important. Don't wait till the end of the night to realize you haven't done much that day.

It's not whether you fall off that's important. It's how quickly you can get back up that determines your success—and that's why it's so important to take those halftime breaks.

Those breaks help you see what actually happened and allow you to get back on track and still have a productive day before it's too late.

Don't let a hectic morning ruin the rest of your day. No one says you have to wait till tomorrow to get a fresh start. You can choose to get a fresh start any time during the day!

Take that quick break and mentally imagine yourself pushing a reset button, and then poof! You're refreshed and feeling like it's a brand-new day! You let go of the past and focused on the very next action.

It's always the *very next* action that determines whether you'll hit your goals and creates your future.

Your success is not determined by how well you react when things go well, but how you react when things don't go as planned. That's the *Experience Formula* that I discussed earlier.

When things don't go well, take a quick one-minute break, let whatever has already happened go, and just focus on the *very next* thing you must do.

Recap the Day and Focus on Getting Just 1% Better

The last part of tracking is to focus on getting just 1% better than you were yesterday.

If you don't focus on what you get better at, it's easy to let your lack of results and negative self-talk discourage you.

Before you go to bed, I want you to recap. Take the Daily EQ Quiz that I shared earlier and pick out *one* thing you got better at that day.

During this time, you should also plan out your activities and the sales prospects that you plan to reach out to the next day.

Tracking requires tools, and you're about to learn the *Consistency Toolbox* that'll help make tracking and staying consistent even easier.

CHAPTER 17

Your Consistency Toolbox

Every one of the successful entrepreneurs that I've interviewed on my MLM Nation podcast declared that consistency is the most important factor in their success, and they always prioritize their checklists of income-producing activities.

However, willpower is not enough.

You stay consistent by using the *Consistency Toolbox* to help you stay focused and increase your productivity.

If you don't use these tools, you'll never achieve the success you want.

1. Journal
2. Calendar
3. Timer
4. Time Tracker
5. Your Checklist
6. Prospect List
7. Reading Apps
8. Gamification
9. Rewarding Activity

Those are your tools in your *Consistency Toolbox*. Let's take a closer look at each one of them.

1) Journal

The most important tool is a journal that tracks your progress and increases awareness of how you're doing.

There are five important purposes for your journal:

1. Plan your week
2. Plan your day
3. See how you're doing in Consistency Huddles
4. Recap your day using the Daily EQ Quiz
5. Write down new ideas

You can use a physical notebook or a digital one. I recommend a digital notebook such as your phone's notepad because it's simple to use. You're always going to have your phone with you. Remember, the first step to being consistent is to make things simple and easy to do!

Even though a physical notebook such as a leather-bound journal is more special, it's less convenient than typing something quickly on your phone. You also don't have to worry about leaving a digital notebook at home or losing it because it's automatically backed up online.

You can always access a digital journal and, as you grow as an entrepreneur, it's cool to be able to go back to your earlier entries to see how you've grown. Physical notebooks run out of paper and then you have to start new ones. If you're looking for something you wrote a while back, you don't want to have to go through old notebooks. A digital journal has all your information in one location and lasts forever.

My favorite journals are my Notes app and Evernote. These apps back up automatically and sync to all devices, and you can access them anytime.

2) Calendar

Many people say I'm the most consistent and productive person they've ever met, and that's because of how strict I am with my calendar.

Every hour of my life is basically blocked off in my calendar, whether it's for business or family activities.

I also go to bed and get up at the same time every day and have a routine for everything.

All the activities in my life are scheduled, and I just go from one activity to another. There's never a moment when I'm wondering what I should do next. Everything is planned out.

When people first hear about my calendar, they say that being a slave to your calendar is no fun and there's no freedom.

But the opposite is true!

It's a paradox, but living your life according to your calendar *gives* you freedom.

It allows you to get what you need to get done so that you have the time to do what you want.

The reason I have had the time to run a business, write three books for my boys, make a documentary, coach youth basketball, coach baseball, and do all these other activities with my children is because of my calendar.

I know I'm human. If I didn't schedule everything in, I would get distracted and would never get anything done.

Everyone has only 24 hours in a day, and it's how you budget and use the few hours you have that allows you to live a meaningful life.

Scheduling has made me more productive with the few working hours I have so that I can spend the rest of each day doing the things I love.

My favorite calendar is Google Calendar. It syncs to all my devices and, unlike a physical calendar, I never have to worry about losing it.

Occasionally, I like to go back a few years and see what I had done in the past. Those events remind me of how much I've grown.

3) Timer

The third most important tool that is related to the calendar is using a timer. It keeps you on track and puts pressure on you to move faster.

If you want to be productive, every task must have an end time—even if your time block is as short as 10 minutes. I generally work in time blocks of 30 and 45 minutes when I have energy in the morning, and shorter blocks of time (10 or 15 minutes) when I'm tired in the afternoon.

We do best when we're under pressure.

Remember when you were a student? When did you write your term papers? If you're like most people, you got them done the night before, at the last minute! (Or if you're like me, you got them done the morning they were due!)

I could never get anything done weeks ahead of time. I would always do it at the very last minute, and I hated it. I would be stressed, and I always promised myself to never let that happen again, but it always happened.

The few times I tried to write my papers ahead of time, I would just sit there for an hour, and the best I could do would be to write two to three sentences. But things change when you get down to the last minute! With pressure, you discover you can get a lot done very quickly!

You see this in sports all the time. A team that has been struggling to score for most of the game can all of a sudden get things going and score tons of points in the last few minutes.

We need pressure, and the timer creates artificial pressure and increases our productivity. When the clock is ticking, you don't have time to multi-task and get distracted. You stay focused.

Even as I'm writing this book, I'm working in a 30-minute time block. I have to get as much writing as I can done during this time before I head out to exercise for 30 minutes.

Without this 30-minute time pressure, I find myself distracted with emails, social media, or thinking about other parts of my life that are not related to writing this book.

When you use a timer, remember to keep the duration short and under an hour or else you won't be able to stay focused. You can work under time pressure for only so long before you get burned out and your mind drifts. Keep it short. I like to "watch a TV episode" and keep it to 30 minutes.

My favorite timers are the ones on my Apple Watch and iPhone. You can find a free timer regardless of what device you have.

4) Time Tracker

People who want to save money often start saving by tracking their expenses. The same applies to those who want to save time. If you want to save time, you have to track it.

You don't really know how you're spending your time until you track it!

How and *where* are you spending your time?

The first time you track your time, you'll be shocked at the time you're spending on certain activities.

This was a big game-changer for me. A few years ago, I started to track my time when I couldn't figure out why my business had stalled. Within one week, I discovered that I was spending way too much time doing administrative tasks and not enough time selling. No wonder my business wasn't growing!

There are different apps that you can use that can break down your time into different categories, such as admin work, selling, and finances. My favorite app, which I've been using since 2015, is Eternity for iOS. I cannot live without it, and it helped me to write this book.

Writing a book can take anywhere from nine months to two years, and it's not easy to give up your time to commit to writing every day.

I found myself not writing enough in the beginning, so what I did was create a separate "book" category in Eternity and set a goal of writing for at least 30 minutes a day. Once I started tracking my time, I was able to finish writing the book.

5) Your Checklist

As you know, making a checklist of the things you have to do in order to achieve your goal is Component 1 of the *Consistency System*.

Having a checklist prevents you from forgetting the important things you have to do in order to reach your goal.

You can print your checklist out, use it as your phone's wallpaper, make it into a poster, or do whatever you want, but make sure you're always looking at it and reminding yourself of what you need to do.

6) Prospect List

Sales and marketing are what keep your business alive, and that's why you should always have a list of your prospects.

A prospect list reminds you that selling is the most important activity you should be doing, especially for any home business that earns less than $100,000 a year.

A home-based business can survive without systems (though it won't be efficient or grow quickly) as long as it has new sales coming in. However, the opposite is not true.

Every business will die if it's not selling every week. You need a constant flow of new sales to give you the money for expenses and to build a team so that you eventually have the time to develop systems.

There are many ways to keep track of your prospects, from a simple notebook to digital options such as spreadsheets and apps.

I recommend a digital prospect list for the same reason I recommended digital journals: because of the ability to save, sync, and access it on any device.

7) Reading Apps

Continued personal development is very important, and I recommend making use of digital books on platforms such as Kindle or Apple's Books app because they make it easy to read.

You'll always have your books with you because you never leave home without your phone. I've personally done tons of reading while I'm sitting in the car waiting for my boys to get off from school or when I'm at my barber.

Keeping your books on your phone also makes it easy to go back and review old books and your notes. Everything is in one place, so you never leave home without any books.

You can also read much more quickly on your phone because digital books make speed reading easier. You don't have to deal with the physical page turning.

At first it may take you some time to get used to reading online, but once you get used to it, you'll never go back.

8) Gamification

The next tool that'll help you stay consistent is something that turns your effort into a fun game.

Use a tool that shows you how many consecutive days you're working on an activity. Create a streak and gamify it.

An example is what you learned earlier: that Seinfeld would mark an "X" on his calendar every day he wrote a joke. After a few days, it became a game, and he wanted to keep the streak of "X" going and not miss a day.

You can use a calendar or an app to do this. One of the best apps I use is called "Streaks," and it has even helped me overcome my sugar addiction. I've never done any drug in my life, but I would consider sugar a drug because once I start eating sweets, I cannot stop! I can eat a gallon of ice cream and get sick and still not want to stop. There have been days where I eat 10 bars of Hershey's dark chocolate and still want more!

I have huge cravings all the time, especially when I'm tired. I'm embarrassed to say that there have been days where I eat a few spoonfuls of ice cream at 5 a.m., then eat a few more bites after walking my dog, Obi, and before you know it, an entire half-gallon is gone by noon!

I've tried many things, but nothing worked until I used Streaks.

Once I started tracking, I was able to go from bingeing on sweets daily to only eating sweets five to 10 times a year, only on holiday occasions.

Making my streak into a game has changed my approach and saved me from my sugar addiction.

9) Rewarding Activity

If you want to survive the entrepreneur roller-coaster, you have to learn to focus on activity instead of results. Results take time and it's easy to get discouraged.

You stay motivated by rewarding your activity.

Let's say you've been prospecting for three straight weeks and haven't gotten a sale yet. You'll get discouraged if you focus on the result, so focus on your activity instead.

You can gamify it and play the calendar game and mark an "X" for every day you send out five sales videos. After you have five "X's" in a row, you can then reward yourself with a nice dinner or buy yourself a small toy.

All of a sudden, your attention is shifted to the rewards of activity and the business becomes more fun and less discouraging.

It's important to keep yourself going because you'll eventually get the results you want.

The Most Important Component of All

I've been doing this for over six years and haven't missed it once.

It takes 60 minutes every month and I'm always busy and "never have time" for it, but I never skip this component.

Why?

Because it is the last and most important component of the *Consistency System*.

What is it?

Accountability.

There are many different levels of accountability, and next, I'm going to share a format that will help you to achieve consistency and business success.

CHAPTER 18

Action through Accountability

Every first Tuesday of the month at 11 a.m., I have a special video call with my friend David B., my accountability partner, scheduled on my calendar.

Sometimes I'm excited for it, but often I'm not—especially during weeks where I'm working on big projects and don't have time. But I always let the calendar "be my boss" and show up for the call no matter how busy I am. Why?

That call is **accountability,** and it's the final and most important component of the *Consistency System*. It's been the key to my success for the last 20 years.

My accountability partner makes sure I do what I said I'd do the previous month. We also share what we've learned, our wins, and things that we need help with.

People often think they need a special routine or willpower to stay consistent, but we're human and fall off track. What we need more than anything is accountability because without it, it's impossible to stay consistent.

Whether you realize it or not, there's always something or someone holding you accountable for every action you take consistently, even something as simple as taking the trash out every week. If you're not doing that, the potential smell of trash in your house holds you accountable, even if your spouse or roommate didn't remind you to take it out!

Get Someone to Hold You Accountable

Remember Component 4 of the *Consistency System,* how we have to choose our environment?

Accountability is a major part of that environment because we always do things better when we work together with others.

Accountability applies to other things as well, such as exercise or developing new habits.

How important are environment and accountability to success?

Which person would have a greater chance of exercising consistently, a person who exercises by herself or someone who meets three of her friends at the gym every day after work?

Having accountability will help you stay consistent!

Our *Purpose Driven Networkers* group is more productive than 90% of distributors in the network marketing profession because they can hop onto Zoom multiple times a week and prospect together with me and other members. *That* is accountability.

I've also worked one-on-one with struggling entrepreneurs who suddenly became consistent and started to get results, because they knew I would hold them accountable by checking in with them every day.

We often procrastinate or take too long to do things when we're alone. Accountability solves that problem and is a tool that'll make you so much more productive.

Different Levels of Accountability

Accountability comes in different forms.

You can have a monthly call with your accountability partner, as I do with mine, or you can have daily one-on-one accountability from a mentor.

You can have group accountability like attending a yoga class, being a part of a business community like *Purpose Driven Networkers*, etc.

How often you get the accountability can vary. It can be daily, weekly, monthly, or quarterly.

The only rule is that your accountability session must be consistent, scheduled in advance, and you must *never* miss a session. I've been doing my monthly calls with my current accountability partner for over six years and we have never missed a month.

It's also important to keep your accountability sessions structured with a specific time limit. If there is no end time and the call goes long, then you won't be motivated or feel the need to do the next call. The *frequency* of the calls is more important than how long the calls are. That's why they must be structured.

The Best Time for Your Accountability Call

Your accountability call *must always be on the same day and at the same time.*

As you've learned in Component 2, Create and Schedule the Time, we are **more consistent** when we do things at a set time.

Consistency becomes hard when there is no scheduled time.

Format for Your Accountability Call

You can decide how long the call will last, but the important part is that it must be structured.

As for the length of the call, if you're doing it monthly, I suggest you do an hour-long call, but it can be shorter if you do it more frequently. You can do a 30-minute call if it's once a week, or a call as short as five minutes if you plan to do it daily.

Here's a format you can follow regardless of how long your call is.

Note that each person speaks on all three parts before the other person shares what's going on with them. That means that if it's a monthly 60-minute call, the first person gets 30 minutes of time before the next person goes. This ensures that the call is not dominated by one person and that each person has their own fair share of time to speak.

Part 1: Share Your Wins and Updates

This is a good time to share what you've learned from your recent experiences, books you've read, helpful tools you've come across, etc.

Always make it a goal to provide value to help the other person. Remember that if your partner doesn't get any value from you, they'll stop being your accountability partner.

Part 2: What Challenges Are You Facing?

What are the things that are holding you back? This is an opportunity for your partner to contribute and give their feedback.

Part 3: Ask Questions and Get Help

With the remaining amount of time left, you can ask for help.

The important thing is that once you decide on a time limit, you need to stick to that time.

Accountability calls often fail because people talk too much, and the call lasts forever—and then no one is motivated to do the next call.

When it comes to accountability, frequency is more important than duration.

Putting the *Consistency System* into Action

To sum it up, these are the seven components to the *Consistency System*. You need to have every one of them in place if you want to achieve a goal.

Component 1: Checklist

You must know exactly what you need to do in order to accomplish your goal.

Component 2: Create and Schedule the Time

How will you have the time to work on the checklist? When will you take action each day?

Component 3: Determine the Strategy

How will you work on each step of the checklist?

Component 4: Choose Your Environment

Where will you be taking action?

Component 5: Tracking

How will you measure your progress and know if you're on track?

Component 6: Your Consistency Toolbox

What tools will you be using that'll help you be more efficient with your action steps?

Component 7: Accountability

Who is going to make sure you stay focused and consistent?

Whether it's a big project or a simple daily task that you're struggling to do every day, the *Consistency System* will help you achieve your goals.

As we wrap up, I'm going to share with you two real-life examples of the *Consistency System* in action that you can apply to your life.

CHAPTER 19

Singing Happy Birthday Every Day!

The *Consistency System* will allow you to achieve all types of goals, whether they're simple things like daily exercise or bigger projects that may take months or years.

Now you get to see two real-life examples of each of the seven components of the *Consistency System* in action and examples of what to do if something fails.

We will start off with a short, simple task that I do each morning. If you do what I'm about to share with you, it'll bring tremendous rewards to your personal and business life.

Singing Happy Birthday Every Day

I'm tone deaf and can't sing for my life. But there is one song that I can sing well, and it's "Happy Birthday"!

Why?

Because I practice singing it at least 10–15 times every day!

Singing "Happy Birthday" to my friends is a routine that has helped me with building relationships and has grown my business.

If you really want to change your life, expand your network, and change how people perceive you, then start singing "Happy Birthday" to every one of your friends, 365 days of the year!

Yes, you read that right. I sing "Happy Birthday" to every one of my friends and Facebook friends on their birthdays, 365 days a year.

I started doing this a couple of years ago. The first year, people I did it with thought I was weird. But, within two years, my whole life changed.

People saw me differently. I gained respect, increased my influence, and got referrals—simply because I took a minute each day to sing someone "Happy Birthday." It makes people happy, and people always remember how you make them feel.

Singing "Happy Birthday" this many times takes about five to 20 minutes a day, and it can get hard to fit it into a busy schedule, but the *Consistency System* helps me get it done.

Component 1: Checklist

Each morning I go to Facebook and it shows me whose birthday is coming up the next day. I also check my phone's calendar, which shows the birthdays of my friends who aren't on Facebook. To do this, you can simply add the birthday in the "birthday" field when you enter a new contact on your phone. After I get the list of birthdays, I write the list of names down on my iPhone's Notes app. That list is my checklist.

Component 2: Create and Schedule the Time

I go through the checklist at 7 a.m. before I go exercise. After I exercise, I walk my dog. That's when I sing "Happy Birthday" to everyone on the checklist.

Sometimes it seems to take forever, especially when I have to do it for 20 people! But the time it takes me is always shorter than my walk with my dog.

Component 3: Determine the Strategy

When I'm walking Obi, I toggle back and forth between the Notes app and my camera to see the list I created and sing to everyone. I *do not* sing and immediately send out the message afterward, because that is like multitasking and would take too much time.

Instead, I batch the task and focus *only* on singing to every single person on the list.

After I get home and feed Obi, that's when I batch send. I toggle between my text and Messenger apps and send out every single message. Afterward, I post on each person's Facebook wall to wish them a happy birthday and to let them know that I sent them a message. This is important, because if I don't do this, they may miss the message. Otherwise, people get so many messages on their birthdays that mine may get buried.

In order to make my message stand out, I always sing "Happy Birthday" a day early so that I'm the *first* person to wish each person happy birthday. This way, my message doesn't get mixed in with all the other greetings they may get.

Component 4: Choose Your Environment

I record the messages in my neighborhood while walking Obi. I send out the messages after I get back home.

I'm sure I have some neighbors who think I'm crazy! Here's this guy holding his dog's leash with one hand, while singing "Happy Birthday" and recording video on his phone with his other hand.

But I don't care what others think because this routine has made me super happy. Not only have I indirectly made lots of money by doing this, but it just also makes me feel good when I make others feel good.

Component 5: Tracking

Every day, I go through the Facebook alerts to make sure I didn't miss anyone.

Component 6: Consistency Toolbox

My personal calendar, Facebook, text app, Facebook Messenger, Notes app, iPhone.

Component 7: Accountability

My coaching clients and children hold me accountable. I teach them to do this and I must set the example.

Facebook also holds me accountable because it reminds me of past and upcoming birthdays every morning.

The people in my life also hold me accountable. Now that everyone knows about this, I can't stop, right?!

Every one of my friends also indirectly holds me accountable. After I sing "Happy Birthday" to them one year, they will feel left out if they don't get a song the next year!

Update the System to Accommodate Different Situations

I'm not perfect, though.

I've been singing "Happy Birthday" to friends every day for years, but there have been a few times I was late to sing for someone.

And do you know why I missed it?!

It's because there was a change in the *Consistency System* and I failed to prepare for it!

The few times I was late to sing "Happy Birthday" happened when I flew out to other cities.

I live in Los Angeles, and I always take the first flight out early in the morning at 5 or 6 a.m. to avoid airport delays. This means I have to leave my house around 3 or 4 a.m., and on those days my wife walks Obi. This means that Component 2 (*Create and Schedule the Time*) and Component 4 (*Choose Your Environment*) change.

Those times that I was late to sing "Happy Birthday," I had found myself saying I would sing birthday songs after I got to the next city, but something always happened once I landed, and I would forget! Without the *Consistency System* in place, we often forget or neglect what we're supposed to do.

After being late to sing birthday songs a few times, I realized I needed to set up a new *Consistency System* for days when I travel.

My travel version of the *Consistency* System is that I prepare the list of people I'll sing to before I leave my house in the morning, and then I sing "Happy Birthday" in my Uber on my way to the airport. I updated Component 2, *Create and Schedule the Time,* and Component 4, *Choose Your Environment,* by singing inside the Uber.

There are plenty of Uber drivers who think I must be one of the weirdest riders they've ever had, but I don't care.

If you want to stay consistent, you must use the *Consistency System!*

How I Wrote This Book

Once you have the seven components of the *Consistency System* in place, you can also achieve any big goal that you set.

This book was a huge project for me, and I've been procrastinating on writing it for years because I knew it would take at least nine months. I found myself always giving the same excuse, "I don't have the time." I was already busy running my company, collecting sports cards, and spending at least 20 hours a week on coaching youth sports.

I also didn't feel like writing, but I made it happen by using the *Consistency System.*

When the project first started, I wasn't consistent because I had to figure out how to create the *Consistency System* to support the writing. I wasn't writing enough and was falling behind schedule. I really dreaded writing and regretted that I had decided to publish a book.

But I'm not a quitter, and I knew that all I needed was the *Consistency System.*

Once I figured out the seven components, I got going and things started to happen. It also became fun, and I looked forward to writing each morning.

This is how I did it:

Component 1: Checklist

I hired a writing coach, and every week, I had specific things I had to do or write.

I also created a checklist of ideas and a to-do list on my Notes app during the editing process.

Component 2: Create the Time

Every morning, Monday to Saturday, I would spend 30 minutes writing immediately after I did my online prospecting session with my *Purpose Driven Networkers*. I would write from 6:25 a.m. to 6:55 a.m.

On Sundays, I would write from 5:30 a.m. to 7 a.m. because I didn't have my session with my *Purpose Driven Networkers*.

I would also write for 30 minutes every weekday, immediately after my morning power nap. This was when I was most alert, with maximum mental energy, and that allowed me to be productive and creative.

In order to create this time, I had to give up on replying to emails and social media in the mornings. I allocated those tasks to the later part of the day, when I wasn't as fresh mentally.

Component 3: Determine the Strategy

I would outline each chapter in the same way I would prepare for one of my training sessions, and then I would write.

Component 4: Choose Your Environment

I wrote this entire book sitting at my desk listening to the same album on Spotify on infinite repeat. The album was "Music to Enhance Intellect & Creativity" by Dr. Mythili, and I always played the same song over and over again.

Once I played that music, I immediately got into the mood to write.

Component 5: Tracking

My writing coach gave me a timetable and deadline for each chapter of the book. I used writing software to track the number of words I wrote.

I also had a goal to spend at least five hours a week on writing, so I tracked how much time I actually spent.

Component 6: Consistency Toolbox

Here is a list of tools I used to write this book:

iPhone Notes

I used this to create my outline, jot down ideas, and create a to-do list for editing.

iA Writer Classic

A very basic writing program that helped me focus on writing. It has zero bells and whistles, such as menus and icons, that could distract me.

Desktop Curtain

This is a software program that covers up your entire desktop so that other files and programs won't distract you. When I used it while writing, the only things that my eyes could see were my manuscript and checklist.

Timer

I used the timer on my watch and gave myself only 30 minutes at a time to write. This reminded me of the other things I had to do (exercise, make breakfast for the kids, walk Obi) and created urgency. It made me write as quickly as possible because I knew I couldn't write anymore once the time was up.

Eternity App

This is a time-tracking app that was extremely helpful. In the beginning, I thought I was committed to the project, but I was wrong!

Thanks to the Eternity app, I discovered I was writing *only* two hours a week. Once I started to track and made sure I wrote for at least five hours a week, I became really productive and the project started to gain momentum.

Component 7: Accountability

Every successful person hires a coach to get them to the next level, so I had to do the same.

I hired a writing and book launching coach who helped me make the project happen. We had a short call every week.

This helped tremendously in the beginning, *before* I apply the *Consistency System*. In fact, it was the only thing that kept me going. I wanted to quit many times, but I knew I had to write something before each weekly call because I didn't want to waste the money I spent on coaching.

The coaching calls kept me in the game until I applied the *Consistency System.*

My monthly accountability partner also pushed me to write even on the days I felt burned out or discouraged.

Getting Back on Track

If you find yourself being inconsistent, go through the *Consistency System* and apply it to the goal you want to achieve.

If you still find yourself occasionally getting off track, don't despair. The reality is that that's going to happen.

The question is how quickly you can get back on track to consistency. That will determine your success. You're about to discover how to win that daily battle.

CHAPTER 20

Winning the Daily War

Even though you've read to the end of this book, I guarantee you're going to screw it up and miss a day!

Why?!

Because you're human!

There are two truths to consistency.

First, no one is born consistent. It's a skill we learn and develop.

Second, no one can stay consistent forever.

No matter how consistent you are, there will be days where life will hit you and you'll get knocked off track.

Aim and expect to be consistent, but don't be surprised if you slack off or have unproductive moments.

Getting off track is going to happen, so don't get down and beat yourself up when it happens. What's important is how quickly you can get back on track.

It's a Daily War against the Devil

Most of success is about your mindset. There are two sides to each of us. You are your greatest supporter, but also your biggest enemy.

Part of you is the Angel, who roots for you and makes you believe that you can accomplish whatever you want. When your Angel is powerful, you're motivated, brave, and willing to do the things you need to do even though you don't want to do them.

Then there is the Devil, who constantly discourages you with negative self-talk and distracts you. The Devil also comes from your DNA, where humans naturally want to take it easy, relax, and only work when we have no other choice. When the Devil is strong, you're filled with self-doubt and your goals seem impossible.

The Angel and Devil are in a constant battle, and, if you want to be consistent, you have to approach each day as a war. It's that intense!

Sadly, for most people, the Devil wins because there's no conscious effort to beat him.

You must wake up each morning ready to defeat the Devil. In fact, your daily goal needs to be to constantly fight and beat the Devil, who's always working hard to get you off track.

The Devil is not easy to beat because he usually gets stronger as the day goes on. Every task you do sucks up your physical and mental energy—and the less you have in your tank, the stronger the Devil is.

That's one of the reasons why you should always work on your checklist when you have the most energy. Get the important things done before the Devil becomes powerful.

The Devil in you is tricky, though. If you don't adopt this all-out war attitude, the Devil will discourage you and get you off track. Before you know it, all your willpower and mental energy will be drained, and you'll waste another valuable day that you can never get back in your life.

When you are off-guard or simply tired, the Devil will win a battle and push you off course.

When this happens, just realize that *you can still bounce back* and have a productive day. **You may have lost the battle, but don't lose the war.**

That's why *Consistency Huddles* are so important. They allow you to assess your day, see what damage the Devil has done, and plan your strategy on how to bounce back.

It's not realistic to win every battle, but you can win the war and have a productive day.

Five Traps That Destroy Consistency

If you want to bounce back more quickly and stay consistent, make sure you avoid these five consistency traps.

1) Feeling Defeated When You Get off Track

Don't be too hard on yourself. Instead, learn to let things go. Instead of thinking about how you messed up, focus on the very next thing you can do to get back on track.

If you focus on the negative, you'll be stuck.

Instead, push that mental reset button, go back to your checklist, and take one small action step that'll get you going in the right direction.

2) Not Doing at Least One Thing Every Day

You must do *something* on your checklist every day for your business.

If you're a new entrepreneur with a part-time business, you actually don't need much time.

No matter how busy you are, you can always take one minute to do something for your business.

It can be as simple as copying and pasting one follow-up message or reaching out to five cold market strangers on social media.

Even on a day when you can't complete your entire checklist, you can always send out one message.

If you don't have much time, you don't need to immediately reply back to every single message you receive. You can always do that later or the next day, but getting the first message out is always the hardest but most important thing to do.

Lost days hurt you because you lose your identity.

Remember, it's about how you see yourself and the person you're becoming. You always act according to your self-concept.

Doing nothing for an entire day also hurts your belief in yourself and your belief in your business.

3) Missing Two Days in a Row

If you happen to screw up and miss an entire day of working on the checklist, let it go and just focus on working on the checklist the next day.

Forget about what just happened. Instead, focus on what you can do to get back on track that very next day.

Never miss two days in a row. One day is an exception, but two days becomes a rule.

Focus on doing the easiest thing on your checklist to get back on track.

4) Bad Environments

If life distractions (such as kids in the house) are making you go crazy, step outside for two minutes and send out one follow-up message.

Even if you don't do anything for the rest of the day, you know you defeated the Devil and were able to do something positive for your business.

5) Negative People

If you're struggling, the worst thing you can do is spend time with negative people.

Don't deal with negative friends, poor prospects, those who discourage you, or people with no ambition.

Protect your mind and your self-esteem and instead listen to something positive and send out a message.

Sending just one message may not grow your business much, but it reinforces your confidence. It proves that you can defeat the Devil and that you're not someone who can be easily defeated.

You may have lost the battle, but you won the war. You did *something*.

How to Get Back on Track

Here's how to quickly bounce back and get back on track.

1) Let It Go

Forget what happened. You just lost a battle but didn't lose the war. Focus your energy to get back on track.

2) Focus on Activity and Not Results

The worst thing you can do is to think about how you messed up and your lack of results.

Always remember that activity will eventually give you results, so take action ASAP.

Taking immediate action also increases your self-esteem and confidence to battle the Devil.

3) Do Something Small

You get back on track by taking a small step in the right direction.

The good news is that you can get back on track *any time*.

It just takes a quick decision to do one small thing and you're good.

4) Focus on Getting 1% Better

If you've been out of it for a while, set a goal to *just get a little better* at your business today.

Send out one more sales message than you did yesterday.

This will compound and give you great results over time.

5) Plan the Day Before

Before you go to bed, make it a goal that you'll win the war against the Devil tomorrow.

Plan out your day and create the intention to stay focused and to get back on track.

Say to yourself that you will do everything you need to do to stay consistent and, finally, visualize yourself winning the day.

6) Take a *Consistency Huddle*

On your first day back on track, take a timeout midday and do a *Consistency Huddle.*

See if you were on track and, if not, make adjustments.

7) Get Accountability

Community and accountability make things happen, and that's why self-help groups emphasize weekly meetings and sharing.

One of the best ways to get back on track is to have someone hold you accountable immediately.

8) Do Short Spurts and then Reward Yourself

If you haven't done much in a while, the worst thing you can do is to go all out immediately.

If you haven't even prospected for five minutes in the last few days, there's no way you can prospect for one hour!

You'll burn out fast, and it'll discourage you from taking action again tomorrow.

Instead, do a short burst of prospecting for five to 10 minutes and then reward yourself with rest before you do another five-to-10-minute session.

Putting It All Together

Congratulations! You now know how to be consistent and bounce back if you've gone off track.

Consistency is a skill that *anyone* can learn, even if you've struggled with it your entire life.

I want to share with you what happened to one of the most inconsistent people I know after he took *The Consistency Pill.*

CHAPTER 21

Take The Consistency Pill

It was a cold Friday in November 2003, and I was excited to do this business presentation.

John was the total opposite of me.

He seemed very outgoing and had the social skills to be successful, so I made sure he was one of the first people I talked to about my business.

We had dinner at Yuka, one of my favorite sushi restaurants on the Upper East Side in New York City, and I remember that I didn't even get to enjoy the meal because I kept thinking about the best time to bring up the business.

I finally did my pathetic sales pitch and was so excited when John said he was interested! He told me to email him some information and that he would look at it over the weekend.

I was so ecstatic that I didn't even remember what we did the rest of that night. We didn't have smartphones back then, so the only thing I was thinking about was how I was going to email him the moment I got home.

I emailed him that night and waited a few days. There was no reply. I finally felt like I couldn't wait anymore, so I emailed him again and was really disappointed when he told me that he hadn't looked at my original email yet.

I checked in with John again a month later. He had finally looked at the information I sent, but told me it wasn't for him.

I was crushed and discouraged.

I had been struggling for months in the business and the one person who I had thought would finally partner with me had said "no.".

Does that sound familiar?

I can relate to you if you're discouraged from your lack of results, because I was a total failure and never made a penny in my first few months.

Fortunately, my business and life changed after I met my mentor, who helped me become consistent.

I started to apply the concepts that I have taught you in this book and the idea that people buy *you*. They buy you and your vision!

I also knew that I didn't necessarily need results for people to partner with me, because people are always buying:

Change
Commitment
Consistency

I never forgot about John, and I would check in with him via AOL Messenger at least once a week to see how he was doing.

We had a few things in common. I'd always start the conversation by talking about the New York Yankees, and then I made sure to let him know about the changes I had made in my life, my commitment to the business, and how I was so excited to be building my empire.

Even though I didn't have many results at the time, nor had I made any money, I made sure John knew about my *change*.

I spent my time reading books and attending business training events instead of wasting my time on things like partying and watching endless hours of TV.

I was also always excited, positive, and enthusiastic about life.

Slowly, over the course of a few months, John started to notice the changes in me until one day he was finally interested in what I did. I immediately connected him with my mentor to help me close the deal.

And yet, John still didn't want to get involved.

The rejection didn't bother me this time because, thanks to my consistent daily actions, I had many other prospects to worry about.

I also knew that there's never a bad prospect, just the wrong time for the right prospect.

The timing wasn't right for John because he was working on a major project at work, but I could tell he was interested.

I just needed to catch him at the right time, so I would continue to follow up with him. I would make sure he always knew about my change, commitment, and consistency.

On a late Friday night after four months of consistent follow-up, I finally got John at the right time.

John had just returned home from a long, frustrating week at work and I could sense that I needed to push for the sale so that I could help him change his life.

I used my *Six-Figure Close,* which consists of these three questions. I would ask each one and wait for him to answer before asking the next question.

1. *Do you want to earn extra income?*
2. *Do you see how our company can help you earn extra income?*
3. *When's the best time to start earning extra income?*

There was a long pause after the third question, and John lightheartedly replied, "Now. You got me!" and laughed. I went ahead and immediately asked for his credit card, and he purchased a business start-up pack that Friday night.

But that's just half the story.

I thought John would be a superstar immediately, because he had good social skills and a big network, but I was totally wrong.

Prospecting is all about timing, and John's friends were at a stage in their lives where all they wanted to do was work a nine-to-five job and party. They had no interest in looking at anything else.

In John's first year, I would visit him in Hoboken, New Jersey, to make sales calls together in his tiny two-bedroom apartment. I could tell John's friends and his roommate all thought I was this crazy dude who got their friend into his "weird" business. In fact, John's girlfriend even refused to help him and wouldn't be a customer because she thought our business was a scam.

But I knew that people always buy your:

Change
Commitment
Consistency

So, eventually, they'd be interested.

You can't convince your prospects. You just outlast them with your consistency.

Every time I visited John, his friends would be in the living room watching TV and hanging out and I would close the door and just make sales calls with John for two hours in his room.

His friends thought we were nuts! I knew they were making fun of us, but we would outlast them with our consistency. I wanted them to see our commitment.

But John was stuck and didn't get any results.

*Six months had passed, and in all that
time, John only made one sale.*

All his contacts rejected him, and John would often get discouraged. There were many times he wanted to quit, but I held him accountable like my mentor had done for me.

My accountability kept John going and going.

Over time, his friends and especially his girlfriend started to see positive changes. John, who would never read a book before, started to read. He would party less, and, more importantly, he started to associate with the top leaders on our team.

Because both of us were focused and committed, we started to see opportunities to get good cheap leads online. This was back in 2004, before there was Facebook, and things were a lot harder, but we decided to become masters at online marketing.

John and I had implemented the *Consistency System* and would work every day for another 30–60 minutes after our prospecting hours on ways to find good cold market leads from the internet.

And that's all we did.

We worked on our checklist first, and after there were no more prospects to reach out to, we would work on internet marketing.

We didn't jump around and do different things. We just stayed consistent doing the same thing every single day.

Many people would say it was boring, but consistency is the secret to success.

We made a lot of expensive online marketing mistakes, but we knew that *consistency creates mastery,* and eventually we would make all the money back.

Every time John was distracted, I was there to get him back on track because I believed that consistency would eventually lead to his success.

We just stayed consistent doing the same thing over and over again.

And then…mastery happened!

After months of struggle, John made six big sales in a three-week span—and even his skeptical girlfriend bought in.

His negative friends saw John's change, commitment, and consistency, and eventually they all either partnered with us or became customers.

As the weeks and months went by, John got busier and busier with his job and part-time business, but the *Consistency System* allowed him to stay consistent with his checklist.

He would follow up with prospects during his lunch breaks and call his sales team to check in on them when he was walking the streets of Manhattan to take the PATH train back to New Jersey.

Often, his prospects and team would hear the sirens and honking from cars on the street, but John didn't care. He knew that consistency creates mastery. There was no stopping him.

While others got bored and did different things, John followed the same routine and stayed consistent.

Two and a half years later, in January, 2007, John surprised his colleagues at his job when he submitted his resignation letter. His consistent efforts had paid off and created freedom. The income from his part-time business had surpassed what he was making at his full-time job, and he no longer needed to work there.

John, who had never left America in his life, immediately went out and traveled around the world to expand his business internationally.

Today, John is a stay-at-home dad and a top business leader and has earned over a million dollars from his part-time business.

More importantly, John is one of my best friends.

People often say that you lose friends in business, but that's only true if you do it the wrong way.

John went from being a colleague who I barely knew to being one of my groomsmen in my wedding. Today he lives three minutes from my house.

I'm sharing this true story with you because this is what can happen to you if you take *The Consistency Pill.*

You'll be the next superstar leader and I'm excited for your future.

Remember, business is about helping others—so, go out there, stay consistent, and have a positive impact on as many lives as possible!

God bless!

Acknowledgments

I'd like to first thank my Lord and Savior, Jesus Christ, who died on the cross for my sins. He has blessed me more than I've ever deserved. Nothing would be possible without Him.

Thanks to my wife, Kelly, for her ongoing love and support. I'm blessed to have Ethan, Brendan, and Christian to inspire me to set an example every day.

Thanks to my parents, who taught me the importance of integrity, hard work, and generosity through their actions.

Thanks to my late grandfather, "Gong Gong," and late grandmother, "Po Po" for teaching me to never give up and to work harder to prove the haters wrong.

Finally, life is a nonstop journey and I'd like to thank all my mentors, accountability partners, and friends who pushed me to reach greater heights, especially Wang Zhizhi, Heidi Ueberroth, Stephanie Schwartz, Julien Segui, Robert G. Allen, Jordan Raynor, Ray Higdon, Dave Block, C.P. Sobelman, Tom Schoenwald, Tom Kearns, Steve Swartz, Dan Brink, the late Mike Ray, Scott McGee, and Alexander Denk.

I've been blessed to have met these people in my life. Without them, this book wouldn't have been possible.

Works Cited

(Ackerman, 2021)
(Businessinsider.com, 2016)
(Comedy Central, 2015)
(Lifehacker, 2019)
(Trello.com, 2018)
(www.SI.com, 2014)

Akshar. "Benefits of Mindfulness and Awareness Meditation." *Entrepreneur*, Entrepreneur, 17 July 2020, www.entrepreneur.com/article/353440.

Berland. "Why Do the Songs from Your Past Evoke Such Vivid Memories?" *Psychology Today*, Sussex Publishers, 2013, www.psychologytoday.com/us/blog/the-athletes-way/201312/why-do-the-songs -your-past-evoke-such-vivid-memories.

Bishop, Greg. "Tom Brady Wants to PLAY 'FOREVER.' with His New-Age Prep, He Might Get Close." *Sports Illustrated*, Sports Illustrated, 10 Dec. 2014, www.si.com/nfl/2014/12/10/tom-brady-new-england-patriots-age-fitness.

Clear, James, editor. *Atomic Habits*, 2018.

Clear, James. "How to Stop Procrastinating on Your Goals by Using the 'Seinfeld Strategy.'" *James Clear*, 4 Feb. 2020, jamesclear.com/stop-procrastinating-seinfeld-strategy.

Gladwell. *Outliers*. 2008.

"If You Fail to Prepare You Are Preparing to Fail." *Quote Investigator*, 9 Sept. 2019, quoteinvestigator.com/2018/07/08/plan/.

Quast, Lisa. "Why Grit Is More Important Than IQ When You're Trying To Become Successful." *Forbes*, Forbes, March 6, 2017, https://www.forbes.com/sites/lisaquast/2017/03/06/why-grit-is-more-important-than-iq-when-youre-trying-to-become-successful/?sh=576ecb367e45.

Snow, Sarah. "How Long Does It Take for Social Media Marketing to Start Paying off?" *Social Media Today*, 21 Sept. 2015, www.social-mediatoday.com/marketing/sarah-snow/2015-09-21/how-long-does-it-take-social-media-marketing-start-paying.

Watson, Kathryn. "Cold Shower Benefits for Your Health." *Healthline*, Healthline Media, 25 Apr. 2017, www.healthline.com/health/cold-shower-benefits.

"What Is Self-Concept Theory? A Psychologist Explains. [2019 Update]." *PositivePsychology.com*, 30 Jan. 2021, positivepsychology.com/self-concept/.

"Why Do the Songs from Your Past Evoke Such Vivid Memories?" *Psychology Today*, Sussex Publishers, www.psychologytoday.com/us/blog/the-athletes-way/201312/why-do-the-songs-your-past-evoke-such-vivid-memories.

Additional Resources from Simon Chan

For free tools, blogs, and videos on how to create consistency, defeat overwhelm, and build a successful business online, visit www.SimonWChan.com.

Purpose Driven Networkers

You can ask me questions and have me help you stay consistent so that you'll get your next customer or sale.

You'll also get a quick daily lesson, stay up to date with the latest online strategies, and have private access to over 1,000 specialized training videos at www.PurposeDrivenNetworkers.com.

1 on 1 Coaching

This is hands-on 1 on 1 coaching where I will help you master personal branding, lead generation, business presentation, the art of closing sales and online duplication.

www.SimonChanCoaching.com

MLM Nation Podcast

Listen to the #1 network marketing podcast that features over 700 episodes with top leaders in the profession.

www.MLMnation.com

About the Author

Simon Chan is a consistency coach and speaker who helps home-based business owners earn a part-time income of at least $1,000 a month by getting them to create consistency, defeat overwhelm, and build a successful business online.

Simon is best known as the host of the MLM Nation Podcast, the #1 network marketing podcast, which features in-depth interviews with over 700 top income earners.

Simon started his entrepreneurial journey in 2003 and built a million-dollar business with over 200,000 distributors by pioneering Online Duplication. He retired from building in 2013 to be a full-time business coach and founded MLM Nation.

SimonWChan

Printed in Dunstable, United Kingdom